ARCHITECTS OF AIR POWER

Other Publications:

LIBRARY OF HEALTH
CLASSICS OF THE OLD WEST
THE GOOD COOK
THE SEAFARERS
THE ENCYCLOPEDIA OF COLLECTIBLES
THE GREAT CITIES
WORLD WAR II
HOME REPAIR AND IMPROVEMENT
THE WORLD'S WILD PLACES
THE TIME-LIFE LIBRARY OF BOATING
HUMAN BEHAVIOR
THE ART OF SEWING
THE OLD WEST
THE EMERGENCE OF MAN
THE AMERICAN WILDERNESS
THE TIME-LIFE ENCYCLOPEDIA OF GARDENING
LIFE LIBRARY OF PHOTOGRAPHY
THIS FABULOUS CENTURY
FOODS OF THE WORLD
TIME-LIFE LIBRARY OF AMERICA
TIME-LIFE LIBRARY OF ART
GREAT AGES OF MAN
LIFE SCIENCE LIBRARY
THE LIFE HISTORY OF THE UNITED STATES
TIME READING PROGRAM
LIFE NATURE LIBRARY
LIFE WORLD LIBRARY

FAMILY LIBRARY:
HOW THINGS WORK IN YOUR HOME
THE TIME-LIFE BOOK OF THE FAMILY CAR
THE TIME-LIFE FAMILY LEGAL GUIDE
THE TIME-LIFE BOOK OF FAMILY FINANCE

ARCHITECTS OF AIR POWER

by David Nevin

AND THE EDITORS OF TIME-LIFE BOOKS

TIME-LIFE BOOKS, ALEXANDRIA, VIRGINIA

Time-Life Books Inc.
is a wholly owned subsidiary of

TIME INCORPORATED

FOUNDER: Henry R. Luce 1898-1967

Editor-in-Chief: Henry Anatole Grunwald
President: J. Richard Munro
Chairman of the Board: Ralph P. Davidson
Executive Vice President: Clifford J. Grum
Chairman, Executive Committee: James R. Shepley
Editorial Director: Ralph Graves
Group Vice President, Books: Joan D. Manley
Vice Chairman: Arthur Temple

TIME-LIFE BOOKS INC.

MANAGING EDITOR: Jerry Korn
Executive Editor: David Maness
Assistant Managing Editors: Dale M. Brown (planning),
George Constable, Thomas H. Flaherty Jr. (acting),
Martin Mann, John Paul Porter
Art Director: Tom Suzuki
Chief of Research: David L. Harrison
Director of Photography: Robert G. Mason
Assistant Art Director: Arnold C. Holeywell
Assistant Chief of Research: Carolyn L. Sackett
Assistant Director of Photography: Dolores A. Littles

CHAIRMAN: John D. McSweeney
President: Carl G. Jaeger
Executive Vice Presidents: John Steven Maxwell,
David J. Walsh
Vice Presidents: George Artandi (comptroller);
Stephen L. Bair (legal counsel); Peter G. Barnes;
Nicholas Benton (public relations); John L. Canova;
Beatrice T. Dobie (personnel); Carol Flaumenhaft
(consumer affairs); James L. Mercer (Europe/South Pacific);
Herbert Sorkin (production); Paul R. Stewart (marketing)

THE EPIC OF FLIGHT

Editorial Staff for *Architects of Air Power*
Editor: Jim Hicks
Designer: Donald S. Komai
Chief Researcher: Lois Gilman
Picture Editor: Robin Richman
Text Editors: Russell B. Adams Jr.,
Thomas A. Lewis
Staff Writers: Gus Hedberg, Glenn Martin McNatt,
Leslie Marshall, Richard W. Murphy, William Worsley
Researchers: Patricia A. Cassidy and Blaine M. Reilly
(principals), Betty Ajemian, Barbara Brownell,
Maria Zacharias
Assistant Designer: Van W. Carney
Editorial Assistant: Stafford L. Battle
Art Assistant: Anne K. DuVivier

Special Contributor: John Neary (text)

Editorial Production
Production Editor: Douglas B. Graham
Operations Manager: Gennaro C. Esposito, Gordon E. Buck
(assistant)
Assistant Production Editor: Feliciano Madrid
Quality Control: Robert L. Young (director), James J. Cox
(assistant), Daniel J. McSweeney, Michael G. Wight
(associates)
Art Coordinator: Anne B. Landry
Copy Staff: Susan B. Galloway (chief), Elizabeth Graham,
Celia Beattie
Picture Department: Rebecca C. Christoffersen
Traffic: Kimberly K. Lewis

Correspondents: Elisabeth Kraemer (Bonn); Margot
Hapgood, Dorothy Bacon, Lesley Coleman (London); Susan
Jonas, Lucy T. Voulgaris (New York); Maria Vincenza Aloisi,
Josephine du Brusle (Paris); Ann Natanson (Rome). Valuable
assistance was also provided by: Nakanori Tashiro, Asia
Editor, Tokyo. The editors also wish to thank: Janny
Hovinga, Wibo van de Linde (Amsterdam); Martha Mader
(Bonn); Judy Aspinall, Karin B. Pearce (London); Felix
Rosenthal (Moscow); Carolyn T. Chubet, Miriam Hsia,
Christina Lieberman (New York); Mimi Murphy (Rome);
Akio Fujii, Katsuko Yamazaki (Tokyo).

THE AUTHOR

David Nevin, the son of a United States Army officer, spent his boyhood on various Army posts and served in the Navy and merchant marine. He began his writing career as a Texas newspaperman and spent a decade on the staff of *Life.* He has written several volumes for Time-Life Books, including *The Pathfinders* in the Epic of Flight series.

THE CONSULTANT *for Architects of Air Power*

Eugene M. Emme obtained his Ph.D. from the University of Iowa with a dissertation entitled "German Air Power, 1919-1939." A former professor at the United States Air Force's Air University, Emme was historian of the National Aeronautics and Space Administration for almost 20 years and has written and edited several books, including *Hitler's Blitzbomber* and *The Impact of Air Power.*

THE CONSULTANTS *for The Epic of Flight*

Charles Harvard Gibbs-Smith, Research Fellow at the Science Museum, London, and a Keeper-Emeritus of the Victoria and Albert Museum, London, has written or edited some 20 books and numerous articles on aeronautical history. In 1978 he served as the first Lindbergh Professor of Aerospace History at the National Air and Space Museum, Smithsonian Institution, Washington.

Dr. Hidemasa Kimura, honorary professor at Nippon University, Tokyo, is the author of numerous books on the history of aviation and is a widely known authority on aeronautical engineering and aircraft design. One plane that he designed established a world distance record in 1938.

10132

For information about any Time-Life book, please write:
Reader Information
Time-Life Books
541 North Fairbanks Court
Chicago, Illinois 60611

Library of Congress Cataloguing in Publication Data
Nevin, David, 1927-
    Architects of air power.
    (Epic of flight)
    Bibliography: p.
    Includes index.
    1. Aeronautics, Military—History. 2. Air power—
History. I. Time-Life Books. II. Title. III. Series.
UG625.N48   358.4'009   80-24449
ISBN 0-8094-3279-X (retail ed.)
ISBN 0-8094-3280-3 (lib. bdg.)
ISBN 0-8094-3281-1

CONTENTS

French Voisin bombers maneuver to evade enemy searchlights during a daring night raid on the German-occupied town of Metz in 1916.

A foretaste of air wars to come

"I wish for many reasons flying had never been invented," declared British Prime Minister Stanley Baldwin in 1935 on learning that Germany had secretly built an air force in defiance of the Treaty of Versailles. Four years later an American correspondent in London echoed Baldwin's misgivings by bluntly concluding: "It is blackmail which rules Europe today, blackmail made possible only by the existence of air power."

Indeed, by the late 1930s air power had dramatically altered the strategic balance in Europe. But the seeds of the new order had been sown in World War I, when fledgling military air forces first emerged as adjuncts to the traditional armed services. Military leaders, doubtful at first of the airplane's utility, soon recognized its value as an aerial scout. And before long, fast fighter planes armed with machine guns were ordered into battle to support the armies of both the Allies and the Central Powers.

But a few farsighted men—notably British Chief of Air Staff Hugh Trenchard, William "Billy" Mitchell of the United States Army's Air Service and an Italian Army colonel named Giulio Douhet—insisted that an air force could undertake independent offensive action in war. Each of them on his own evolved a doctrine of strategic air power based on the ability of long-range bombers to attack industrial and transportation centers far behind the enemy's front lines. The flying machines of their day were primitive and could carry only a relative handful of bombs, but these architects of air power foresaw that in an era of total warfare civilians as well as soldiers would become targets of aerial attacks aimed at crushing their will to resist.

Although World War I set the stage for these developments, the concept and use of strategic bombing came too late to shorten that war or to produce decisive effects on land or sea operations. But the bombers' forays were lessons for, and a foretaste of, the future. Shown here in vivid paintings by combat artists—some of whom were skilled aviators who participated in the events they portrayed—these early aerial offensives were grim portents of the awesome destructive might that bombers would unleash in wars still to come.

Royal Naval Air Service flying boats defending Britain's vital sea lanes bomb a German submarine caught on the surface near a merchant convoy.

German planes and barracks erupt in flame during a 1917 Allied night raid on Bissheghem airfield. A parachute flare (center) lighted the target.

Lumbering over enemy territory in 1918, British D.H.4 bombers keep a tight formation to concentrate fire against a swarm of German fighters.

1
Prophets of the new power

There is no place where a woman and her daughter can hide and be at peace. The war comes through the air, bombs drop in the night. Quiet people go out in the morning and see airfleets passing overhead—dripping death—dripping death.''

Thus H. G. Wells, in a fanciful flight of fiction published in 1908, envisioned an apocalyptic *War in the Air* bringing destruction and terror to women and children in peaceful cities far from the battle lines. It was a vision of astonishing prescience in a world in which few had seen machines in flight. Wells had foretold in his fiction a reality that no government had yet perceived—that warfare would be changed, profoundly and forever, by mankind's mastery of the air.

It was, in 1908, a feeble mastery. In May of that year two of the world's most accomplished aviators, French designer Gabriel Voisin and pilot Léon Delagrange, went to Rome to show a large crowd that included the Italian Minister of War what their famous Voisin flying machine could do. It was a poor show. Fighting nasty winds in his crude motorized box kite, Delagrange was able to manage only a few short hops at an altitude of about three feet. The disappointed crowd turned ugly, and police had to use force to escort the aviators to safety and prevent the destruction of the machine. "The reaction of the mob," wrote a French reporter who was present, "in all countries and in all times, has been one of ignorance and brutality in the face of progress."

Yet in the crowd that day one man—a 39-year-old major in the Italian Army named Giulio Douhet—saw what had happened not as an embarrassing failure but as a preview. "Since the airplane is already capable of rising a few feet," he said shortly after the debacle at Rome, "soon it will be able to rise thousands of feet and cover a distance of thousands of miles." What permitted him to see such prospects where others saw only the uncertain staggerings of a flimsy contraption no one can say; he had already been musing for three years about the application of this new device to warfare, and his ideas would trigger a titanic clash of prophecies that would polarize military thinking for decades.

In the summer of that same year, half a world away, a young United States Army officer at Fort Myer, Virginia, encountered one of the men who had started it all: Orville Wright, who was getting ready to demonstrate that the flying machine he and his brother had invented could be useful to the United States Army. The young officer, whose Signal Corps training had included what little was then known about aeronau-

Sir Hugh Montague Trenchard, here resplendent in his dress uniform as Chief of Air Staff, is acknowledged as the great architect of the British Royal Air Force. A man of extraordinary energy, he was aptly described by one admirer as a "natural organiser, a very strong personality and an unrivalled leader of men."

tics, was intrigued. Wright explained the principles of the machine to him and as they discussed its prospects they became good friends.

The officer went on to other assignments and his chance encounter with the pioneer aviator did not then seem to be the stuff of history. But the seed planted by the meeting was to bear bitter fruit in the officer's life; it would alter the military history of his country and the world with all the sudden force of the bombers with which his name—William "Billy" Mitchell—was to become indelibly linked.

The uncertain prospects of flying machines improved measurably during the next year, 1909. Europe's capitals were astounded by the ability of the visiting Wilbur Wright's airplane to stay aloft for unheard-of lengths of time and to maneuver adroitly as no European machine could. The vigorous and rapidly developing aviation industry of France was displayed in a stunning exposition at Rheims. And a French machine electrified political and military strategists in July when Louis Blériot struggled aloft from the French coast in a windy gray dawn, sputtered along at uncertain altitudes, got lost in fog and headed for a time in the wrong direction, but finally shuddered to earth in a barely controlled crash—on English soil. He had crossed the English Channel, the moat that kept Great Britain safe, and had signaled the eventual obsolescence of the island nation's then-invincible sea power.

Press accounts of this marvel spread across the world, reaching Lagos, Nigeria, a month later. There they sparked a conversation between two officers of Britain's South Nigeria Regiment—Lieutenant Colonel Hugh Trenchard and one of his few close friends, Captain Eustace Lorraine. "This flying business is something I must find out more about," said Lorraine. But the 36-year-old Trenchard, after reflecting whimsically on the effect flying machines might have on the superstitious, primitive inhabitants of the Nigerian bush, was uninterested. Ironically, the world was to hear little more of Lorraine, while Trenchard was destined to lead and inspire the world's first independent air force.

Certainly there was little in these events to influence the policies of nations, which are seldom prompted to immediate action by the insights of novelists or visionaries. And rightly so; while H. G. Wells was breathtakingly accurate in predicting the realities of strategic bombing, the fighter planes in his novel flew by flapping their wings; and while Douhet is lauded for those of his conclusions that hindsight finds correct, a reading of his work reveals almost as many that were wrong.

Even in the presence of revolutionary technical change, the response of armies and nations is slow. Almost 400 years passed after the invention of gunpowder before its use in muskets drove the pike and the long bow from the battlefield. Now a few visionaries were about to urge their countries to prepare for just as profound a change in warfare and world politics, one that would see the ages-old domination of battle by armies and fleets ended by something called air power.

"Air power," broadly defined as the extension of military power through the air, was a deceptively simple term that immediately began

Giulio Douhet, the visionary who predicted the future of air power, cuts a jaunty figure in the cock-feather hat of Italy's Bersaglieri, a special mechanized battalion. He served as commander of this elite unit from 1905 until 1912, when he was given command of the Aviation Battalion.

Planes swarm across the cover of this 1918 work by Douhet titled How the Great War Ended—the Winged Victory. *In the text, a fictional American pilot, captured by the Germans, introduces many ideas about air power that Douhet later expanded in his* Command of the Air.

to engender endless questions. Who should control this power? The army, with its traditional role as the primary force in battle? The navy, whose application of sea power more closely paralleled the presumed characteristics of air war? Or should air power be in the hands of a third command, an independent air force? Should air power be used tactically, to win the immediate battle, or strategically, against the resources of the enemy country itself? What weapons could this new technology deploy and which could it use best?

Before any concept of air power could become a reality, those in authority had to define it, understand it and risk their careers by guiding it through the tortuous process of debate that precedes government action. Then there would remain the challenge of developing and assembling the necessary technology and manpower—and of obtaining the huge amounts of money to pay for them. When all that had been done, air power—the theoretical concept hand in hand with the physical weapon—would smash across the 20th Century like a hurricane.

But the dreamers came first. Those whose vision was eventually confirmed were honored, usually posthumously, while their fellow dreamers who were facing the wrong direction were forgotten. Only when the nations of the world had finally hammered out their reactions to the newfound ability of man to fly into battle could anyone know which of the far-flung scouts on the frontiers of military aviation deserved honor. These would include England's Hugh Trenchard, America's Billy Mitchell, Germany's Hans von Seeckt and Erhard Milch, and the Soviet Union's Nikolai Zhukovsky and Andrei Tupolev. But the first man to investigate the unfamiliar terrain of the age of air power was Giulio Douhet of Italy.

For many generations the Douhet family had maintained a tradition of military service to the House of Savoy. The Battaglia family had an equally strong tradition of passionate journalism. It was not surprising, then, that the son born in 1869 to the elder Giulio Douhet and his wife Giacinta Battaglia became a career Army officer who was also a talented poet and playwright and frequently a thorn in the sides of his superiors. By 1909, the younger Giulio Douhet had become adept at presenting his ideas and cared not whom they might offend. He had written two significant books on the mechanization of war, an achievement that made him somewhat suspect in the minds of senior officers: Men who were expert in the deployment of horse cavalry found him altogether too clever, too theoretical and too little interested in regular duty.

Douhet was given command of a special motorized unit, but the high command was not interested in the ideas about the military uses of airplanes he was beginning to express; it had already decided that the future of military aviation lay with dirigibles. None of this deterred Douhet. He had seen only three airplanes—including the Voisin that Delagrange barely got off the ground in Rome—and he had never flown, but he had intuitively recognized the future of air power. He wrote an article for a military newspaper that was stunningly prophetic. In a few words he explained the nature of the new weapon. First, with a detailed and closely reasoned argument, he predicted that the air weapons of the future would be airplanes, not dirigibles. Then he wrote: "To us who have until now been inexorably bound to the surface of the earth, it must seem strange that the sky, too, is to become another battlefield no less important than the battlefields on land and sea. For if there are nations that exist untouched by the sea, there are none that exist without the breath of air.

"Today we are fully aware of the importance of having command of the seas; soon command of the air will be equally important, for the advantage of aerial observation and the ability to see targets clearly can be fully exploited only when the enemy is compelled to remain earth-bound. The army and navy must recognize in the air force the birth of a third brother—younger but none the less important in the great military family."

In embryo form, the central concepts were all there: the quantum leap to total war, implied in the idea that the air, bathing all nations equally, would become a battlefield extending far beyond front lines and national borders; the basic purpose of the new weapon, drawn from lessons learned at sea and summed up in that enduring phrase, "command of the air"; and the recognition of the crucial role of the air weapon in war, not as an adjunct to land and sea forces but as a separate organization with a mission of its own.

But the life of a prophet is not easy. Douhet's ideas brought no reaction from the Italian general staff, although Italy did become the first nation to take the airplane to war. In 1910 the Army purchased a few aircraft as an experiment. The next year Italy fell into a brief conflict with Turkey and invaded Libya, at that time a Turkish colony. After some hesitation, the Italian Army sent along its nine-airplane flotilla.

The world's first combat reconnaissance flight began at 6:19 a.m. on October 23, 1911, when Captain Carlo Piazza took off from Tripoli and flew along the road to Azizia. He was back at 7:20 a.m. with a report on enemy troop placements. The first bombing mission took place on November 1, when a pilot dropped four bombs on Turkish troops. Each was exploded by a grenade after the pilot pulled the pin with his teeth and dropped the four-pound package over the side. Early the next year Captain Piazza borrowed a camera, took it aloft and originated aerial photographic reconnaissance. And air war came full circle when Turkish troops shot down an Italian plane with rifle fire.

The Army was sufficiently impressed by the achievements of its airplanes to form an aviation battalion. Douhet commanded this unit for a time but soon ran afoul of his superiors again. Without authorization, he commissioned a friend, designer Gianni Caproni, to build a three-engined, 300-horsepower bomber that was years ahead of its time. Although the aircraft eventually tested successfully—the War Ministry was to send 40 of them to the front during the first year of World

War I—Douhet's unauthorized approval of the prototype gave his enemies the weapon they needed. Stung by his incessant criticisms and irritated by his single-minded advocacy of air power, they used this infraction as an excuse to remove him from command of the Aviation Battalion and post him to an infantry division.

Douhet soon handed his foes another, more destructive, weapon to use against him. A stinging memorandum in which he detailed military shortcomings and predicted disaster was made public after the outbreak of the Great War. This time he was court-martialed and imprisoned for a year. Soon after his release the very kind of catastrophe he had predicted occurred when the Austro-German forces broke the Italian line at Caporetto. The awful bloodletting that followed—there were 600,000 casualties—was the worst disaster in Italy's military history. Although exonerated by events, Douhet found that he still could not influence military planning as he wished. Eight months after his release from prison he resigned from active service and devoted himself to writing.

It was then that Douhet produced the definitive book, *Command of the Air,* that assured his place in history as the first prophet of air power. Published in 1921, it was a detailed, carefully formulated set of theories for understanding, organizing and conducting the war of the future.

He believed that improved firepower could stop any army and that therefore any future land battle would result in a stalemate precisely like the one that had characterized the recently ended World War I. Only the airplane, he argued, had the freedom to disregard the front lines, take the offensive and inflict total war on the enemy. The next war would be won, he said, by the country that seized and held complete command of the air—that is, the ability "to prevent the enemy from flying and at the same time to guarantee that faculty for yourself."

Bombers must destroy the enemy air force on the ground, he said, and then "inflict upon the enemy attacks of a terrifying nature to which he can in no way react." He specified the use of a mixture of high explosives, incendiaries and poison chemicals so destructive that it would not be necessary for the bombers to strike the targets again. The attack should be massive, using all available bombers, and sudden, with no fighter protection and no regard for enemy defenses. "We must resign ourselves," he wrote, "to the attacks that the enemy may inflict on us so that we may devote all available resources to attacks of even vaster proportions."

In the first edition of *Command of the Air,* which appeared in 1921, Douhet admitted that while the army and navy would have inferior, defensive roles, there would be a need for what he called "auxiliary aviation" to serve their tactical needs and for fighter aircraft for limited defensive roles. But in the second edition, in 1927, he retracted those qualifications and proposed one independent air force flying a "battle-plane"—an armed bomber that he believed could on its own win any war before the armies and navies had time to engage.

It takes nothing from Douhet's genius that many of his premises were wrong. Civilian morale did not crumple under bombardment as he had predicted; ground conflict did not lead inevitably to stalemate; defensive air war, especially after the invention of radar to spot attacking aircraft, remained vital; and the all-purpose battleplane he envisioned was never to emerge. But in his central theme he went unerringly to the heart of the matter: Air power would change warfare and the world.

Thus Douhet stands at the head of a procession of men who would seize the immense idea of what the airplane could mean to war. The other early architects of air power did not necessarily follow Douhet's lead—his ideas were little known outside Italy until *Command of the Air* was published after World War I, and even then a decade passed before it was translated into other languages. Instead his fellow prophets developed their thoughts independently, applying their imaginations and analytical minds to the growing evidence of the need to rethink military strategy to include the new machines.

Hugh Montague Trenchard, like Douhet, grasped the nature of the air weapon and the realities of air warfare remarkably early. But unlike the intellectual Italian, the thoroughgoing Englishman came to his understanding not with an intuitive flash enlarged by abstract logic but through practical reasoning based on long experience in war. Most of the time a reticent man of dark moods and unpredictable reactions, Trenchard was never shy about proclaiming or defending his concepts. His legacy is not an elegant body of theoretical writings such as Douhet left but a collection of specific, pragmatic responses to situations as they arose—responses whose sometimes immoderate vocal force earned him the nickname Boom—that were recorded in his orders, memorandums, speeches and the memories of his colleagues.

As a boy, Trenchard had been a poor student. He failed to qualify for the Royal Military Academy, but he managed in 1893 to achieve the rank of lieutenant in the British Army through service in the militia. A tall, gangling, awkward man, his face already craggy, he was posted to India, where he took up polo with passionate interest. The sport led to his first encounter with Winston Churchill—and an uncertain beginning to a lifelong friendship. Trenchard's Royal Scots Fusiliers polo team met Churchill's 4th Hussars at Ambala. Equally aggressive, the two men clashed frequently as the game progressed. Once, as they closed, Churchill's mallet fell across the neck of Trenchard's horse.

"Play to the rules," Trenchard roared angrily, "and take that stick out of my eye." Glaring, Churchill tried to ride Trenchard off the field and found him unmovable. Finally the straining horses stopped, shoulder to shoulder.

"Who the devil were you talking to?" Churchill shouted. In response, Trenchard knocked Churchill's loosely held mallet from his hand and galloped off. Later they laughed about the incident—a little. Neither man took well to being pressed.

Then in 1900 Trenchard was off to the Boer War in South Africa,

Astride a polo pony at his first post in India, 20-year-old Hugh Trenchard exhibits an aura of authority. The leadership and riding skill he demonstrated at polo caused his superiors to give him command of a mounted battalion in the Boer War.

Defying all medical odds, Trenchard stands beside trophies he won in the 1901 Cresta Run bobsled races at St. Moritz, Switzerland. Paralyzed by a war wound, he miraculously regained the use of his legs in a sledding crash a week before the meet.

where, leading an assault, he took a bullet through a lung. The wound cost him the use of the lung and his legs. Trenchard, who distrusted doctors and hated illness with a near-neurotic intensity, refused to yield to his infirmity. He went to Switzerland and began bobsledding, racing down the slopes and taking wild spills. After a particularly violent crash he found that he could walk again—the impact had corrected whatever had caused the paralysis. He stayed in Switzerland long enough to win the 1901 Cresta Run at St. Moritz and then returned to South Africa. There he resumed command of his cavalry unit, ignoring the fact that he often fell from his saddle in a dead faint and that each day he bled internally. Implacably he advanced to health and the rank of major, earning a reputation as a tough man in a tight spot.

Within a decade, however, Trenchard's career seemed to have reached a dead end. He was rotting away on garrison duty when the friend who had become interested in flying after Blériot's Channel flight in 1909, Captain Eustace Lorraine, wrote him: "You've no idea what you're missing. Come and see men like ants crawling." The phrase caught Trenchard's imagination. It was 1912 and in six months he would be 40, the cutoff age for transfer to the RFC—the new Royal Flying Corps, which accepted only qualified pilots. Trenchard, who had never been in an airplane, took leave and presented himself at T. O. M. Sopwith's flying school at Brooklands, near London. As he arrived he learned that Lorraine had just been killed in a crash. Thirteen days later, with an hour and four minutes of flying time to his credit, Trenchard received Pilot's Certificate No. 270 and set out for the RFC's new Central Flying School.

Britain at this point was far behind France, Germany and the United States in aeronautical development. The British War Office had tried to buy a plane from the Wright brothers in 1906, but the Treasury had blocked the funds and the first recorded flight in England was not made until 1908. After Blériot flew the Channel, Britain suddenly awakened to the airplane with a burst of civilian flying.

But the Army was slow to get interested. Lieutenant General Sir Douglas Haig, former director of the War Office, obviously had not yet seen the light when he said in 1911: "Flying can never be of any use to the Army." But Churchill, who became the minister in charge of the Navy that year, had a higher regard for the potential of flight and instituted a tiny fleet air arm. The government appointed a committee headed by Brigadier General David Henderson to study British air policy. Henderson, a reconnaissance specialist, grasped the airplane's value as a scout for ground forces, though he saw no further possibilities for it. The result of his study was the formation of the Royal Flying Corps under Henderson's command in April 1912. The corps included an Army wing, a Navy wing and a central flying school for both services.

Trenchard presented himself at the school in time for the first class in August. He was a mediocre pilot, but the school's commander—a Navy man—wanted an experienced Army officer on his staff, and to

Trenchard's surprise the school not only accepted him as a student but at the same time made him its adjutant. Finding himself responsible for examinations, Trenchard set up tests, took them, reviewed his scores, decided that he had passed and awarded himself his wings.

British maneuvers in 1912 provided Trenchard with an indelible picture of what the airplane could mean to war. He flew as an observer for a force opposing troops led by General Haig. Scarcely was he off the ground before he saw Haig's troops advancing where they were least expected. He hurried back to inform his general, who had just sent his cavalry in the wrong direction. Trenchard offered to take new orders by air and minutes later he delivered a message to the cavalry column.

Later he remembered how vulnerable the cavalrymen looked—and how far out of place they were. He realized that no commander could operate effectively without the help of the airplane's speed and panoramic view. The orders delivered by Trenchard allowed the cavalry to stop Haig's advance, but a full year later Haig gave clear evidence of his

Hugh Trenchard (middle row, far right) and his fellow officers in the first course at the Central Flying School in Upavon, England, line up behind their mascots for a group portrait in 1912. The school trained pilots for the Army and the Navy.

continued resistance to aviation. "I hope none of you gentlemen is so foolish," he told his officers in 1914, "as to think that the aeroplane will be usefully employed for reconnaissance purposes in war."

When Europe went to war in August 1914, Henderson took to France the 44 aircraft that represented the operational combat strength of the RFC's Army wing (the Navy wing had about 100 planes, half of them seaplanes limited to fleet duty). Britain's lack of foresight now imposed cruel penalties. Germany entered the War with some 700 aircraft. France had at least 500 planes, as did Russia.

Having aircraft available was one thing, knowing what to do with them another. In the crucible of battle the evolution of the new weapon accelerated beyond the ability of most military men to keep up. While pilots were still lofting grenades overboard onto the heads of enemy troops, designers were already at work on bombers that could mechanically unleash hundreds of pounds of high explosive. Groping for the most effective application of air power, some planners would soon conclude that the airplane's greatest value lay in its unprecedented ability to reach far to the rear of the battle lines to disrupt the enemy's capability and will to wage war. But from the beginning that concept, the strategic use of air power, was opposed by others who wanted to apply air power tactically, attacking the men and machines involved in whatever battle was at hand. Tension between these two ideas would dominate military affairs for decades, but that contest would come later. As the War began, the airplane's only recognized role was that of an unarmed scout.

The RFC operated cautiously in the fluid opening days of the War. Its first triumph came when a British pilot over France spotted the German II Corps sweeping around the flank of the unsuspecting British forces. Reinforcements prevented a major disaster, and within a month the fighting settled into static trench warfare. The RFC's observation techniques began to improve, but German aircraft had free run of the skies and were giving devastating direction to German artillery.

Trenchard, busy in England pressing civilian aircraft and aviators into the service, fumed at reports of problems at the front, but radiated admiration for a few early bombing raids. These were made by British naval aircraft. In September, four Navy planes took off from Antwerp to attempt the first bombing raid on Germany. Only one of them made it to the Düsseldorf airship sheds that were the target; only one of the four bombs it dropped exploded—and that one missed. Early in October two Sopwiths dropped a few 20-pound bombs on the railroad station in Cologne, doing little damage, and on the Düsseldorf airship sheds, where they had more success. Later that year they would hit Friedrichshafen and Cuxhaven airship facilities even more effectively, but it was the idea, rather than the results, that Trenchard was enthusiastic about.

When Henderson visited England in October, Trenchard upbraided him for contenting himself with patrolling—as Trenchard put it, "wrapping his machines and pilots in cotton-wool." Henderson, an even-

Sir David Henderson, Britain's Director-General of Military Aeronautics from 1913 to 1918 and a close friend and admirer of Hugh Trenchard, helped found and develop Britain's Royal Flying Corps.

tempered man, merely protested that British observation had been excellent. Not enough, Trenchard thundered; Britain would never gain ascendancy in the air while enemy pilots had the initiative. British aircraft must attack the enemy's airfields, destroy his planes on the ground, seize and hold command of the air. He finished in a blaze of anger, demanding to be relieved of air duty and returned to his regiment.

Instead, Trenchard's patient chief sent him to an air command in France. Henderson had divided his air forces into three wings, one attached to each British army. Trenchard took command of the First Wing and reported in January of 1915 to the redoubtable Sir Douglas Haig. It was a meeting Trenchard dreaded, for Haig was an awesome figure and his negative attitude toward aviation was well known. But something in Trenchard's direct manner seems to have intrigued Haig, for at this meeting they began a working relationship that soon blossomed into friendship and trust. Haig wanted to know what role aircraft were going to play in the future. Trenchard said that they would have to do more than observe: They would have to fight in the air against German machines—and they would need not only machine guns but bombs.

Haig then revealed that a major offensive was planned for March. He wanted to know what the First Wing could do. While Trenchard was not yet able to attack the Germans, he was ready to expand the role of his airplanes beyond simply watching the enemy. By using visual signals and the crude radios that were just then being tried out, Trenchard said, aircraft could direct artillery fire. The prospect intrigued Haig, and he said he wanted to know in advance if bad weather would ground the planes. "If you can't fly," he said, "I shall probably put off the attack." Trenchard was elated. Haig was finally making use of the air weapon.

Before the engagement—which would be remembered as the Battle of Neuve-Chapelle—the first British photoreconnaissance unit provided detailed pictures of the enemy positions. On the fateful morning, Haig launched his initial bombardment only when told visibility was adequate. But the attack went badly, and by the end of the day the British troops were reeling back. Trenchard went from base to base talking to his returned pilots, thus initiating the practice of debriefing that would become standard in all air forces. What he learned was discouraging: The artillery barrage had been less effective than expected, partly because British gunners had ignored his spotters' signals.

When Trenchard visited artillery units to protest, one commander told him, "Don't you see that I'm far too busy fighting to have time for playing with your toys in the air?" Haig, now fully converted, assembled his artillerymen to tell them he intended to use the air weapon and that those who did not agree would be replaced. Although the attack at Neuve-Chapelle failed, Haig's message eventually got through, and at the battle for Loos in September the partnership worked effectively.

Haig succeeded to command of all British forces late in 1915, and Trenchard, promoted to general, took command of the RFC. Maurice

Winston Churchill (in the flying helmet) is greeted at his landing site after a flight from Upavon to Portsmouth in 1915. Although he was a most effective political advocate of air power, Churchill's style as a pilot was criticized by Trenchard, who described it as "wallowing about the sky."

Baring, a British poet and intellectual who spoke eight languages, became Trenchard's aide. "Take a note of that, Baring," Trenchard would say as he and Baring moved from base to base, poking, probing, asking questions, gathering complaints, sensing and solving problems.

Baring's tact served Trenchard well, both in preserving excellent relations with his French counterparts and in translating Trenchard to his own men. Trenchard relied on the expressive grunt when he had nothing better to say, which was often. But when he did speak he tended to blast, and Baring's easy way with language tempered Trenchard's blunt declarations, clarified his ideas and made his writing persuasive.

Trenchard's belief in attack at all costs sometimes made him seem brutal. Sending a pilot on a desperate attempt to knock down a German observation balloon in a key position, Trenchard said, "Good luck, but remember this: It's far more important to get that balloon than to fail and come back." But when he caught an overzealous officer punishing mechanics with a cross-country run before breakfast, he roared, "This is a technical corps. You're not in the Army now, you know."

The men of the RFC began to share an affectionate respect for their rough-tongued chief as they told one another stories of his singular behavior. He visited London at the height of two curious phenomena of the War—a spate of unwed mothers with unwanted war babies, and a corps of women who took it upon themselves to berate men whom they suspected of slacking in the war effort. Men wore silver badges to signify employment in essential war work. Trenchard had donned civilian clothes and was sitting in the park in momentary relief from command when he was accosted by a waspish woman who demanded, "May I ask you, sir, where is your war badge?" Trenchard glared at her. "May I ask you, Madam," he snapped, "where's your war baby?"

Trenchard's fliers needed a leader whom they could admire, who was as tough as they had to be. For the War had turned foul and hopeless as the armies found themselves locked in a deadly stalemate along hundreds of miles of trenches. Then the fighter duels began, and the air war seized the public imagination; its gallantry seemed proof of the worth of the individual denied by the brutish combat in the mud below.

But to Trenchard, fighter duels were not the air war; they were a reaction to the air war, which really consisted of attacking the enemy on the ground. In his view it was the observation planes, the artillery spotters, and the bombers hitting enemy air bases, railways and troop concentrations that made the air weapon felt. The hard realities of war were proving Trenchard's conviction that the airplane was a superb offensive weapon—and that to use it primarily for defense was a fatal error. Even against the new Fokker, Trenchard maintained the offensive. He massed his aircraft to get the maximum effect from each attack, developed formation tactics, sent fighter planes to escort bombers—but in order to maintain the attack, he accepted casualties that sometimes ran to 50 per cent each month. "The hardest thing in war," he would say, "is to discover commanding officers of sufficient calibre not to mind losing men when the goal is worth the sacrifice."

What the RFC was fighting for was command of the air—the ability to carry out a mission and to prevent the enemy from carrying out a countermission. The German forces, even with superior numbers and equipment, concentrated on making British probes extremely expensive rather than counterattacking to break the RFC's hold on the air by destroying British bases. A German general later observed that the fighting in 1916 "was marked by a complete inferiority of our own air force. The enemy's airplanes enjoyed complete freedom. With the aid of airplane observation the hostile artillery neutralized our guns." His own planes, he added, rarely broke through for reconnaissance.

Trenchard expected the enemy to respond in kind and try to seize the air initiative. He dreaded the demands that British ground forces would then make for RFC protection against enemy airplanes. In late 1916, defending in advance against such demands, Trenchard wrote, with Baring's help, one of the earliest analyses of air power.

"Owing to the unlimited space in the air, the difficulty one machine has in seeing another, the accidents of wind and cloud," he wrote, "it is impossible for aeroplanes to prevent hostile aircraft from crossing the line if they have the initiative and determination to do so. The aeroplane is not a defense against the aeroplane, but as a weapon of attack cannot be too highly estimated." The enemy's use of the air had been basically defensive, he said, noting that it was Britain's offensive strategy that forced the enemy "to keep back or to detail portions of his forces in the air for defensive purposes." But Trenchard continued to expect that the Germans would try to seize the offensive. Eventually they did.

In the spring of 1917, thirty new Gotha G.IV bombers, massive twin-engined biplanes, each capable of carrying 1,100 pounds of bombs to England, were assigned to the German Air Force's Heavy Bomber Squadron 3. The German command looked to the Gothas to do what two years of largely ineffective bombing by Zeppelin airships had failed to do—divert British fighters from the front to the defense of London and thus ease the tactical pressure of Trenchard's constant attacks.

In May, 21 Gothas bombed Folkestone on the Dover coast, killing 95 civilians. On June 13 a flight of 17 Gothas droned over London "serenely, insolently and practically with impunity," as an air vice marshal later said. They dropped nearly two tons of bombs in two minutes. One bomb smashed into the Upper North Street School, killing 18 children and wounding 30. All told, 162 people were killed and 432 were injured. The Gothas were untouched by British fighters or antiaircraft fire.

The humiliation made a bad time worse for the British. The war of attrition was killing their young men in ever greater numbers. French troops had mutinied and British troops were angry. Russia, consumed by revolution, was out of the War, and while the United States had come in, its power could be applied only slowly. The German submarine campaign was tightening a noose around England's neck. And now there were bombers over London.

A member of the War Cabinet, the brilliant South African lawyer, politician and soldier General Jan Christiaan Smuts, was ordered to analyze the situation. After a quick study Smuts issued a report with historic consequences. Britain not only should respond in kind by bombing German civilians, he concluded, but should regard such a strategy as essential to modern warfare. "The day may not be far off," Smuts wrote, "when aerial operations with their devastation of enemy lands and destruction of industrial and population centers on a vast scale may become the principal operations of war, to which the older forms of military and naval operations may become secondary and subordinate." The War Cabinet seized the idea, created a separate air ministry—equal to rather than subordinate to those of the Army and Navy—and approved a bombing campaign designed to blast Germany out of the War.

Trenchard, engrossed by the Herculean task of building an air force while at the same time meeting the demands of combat, was contemptuous of the serpentine Whitehall plotting that had led to constant shifts

Low-flying French planes spread terror and destruction through enemy trenches in this painting from the cover of a 1918 Italian magazine. Proof of a growing regard for the military value of aircraft, such bombing raids were cited as crucial to the Allies' successful advance across France.

Between flights, German airmen check out their Gotha G.V bomber, a pusher biplane with two engines and an 77-foot wingspan. A witness of the Gothas' 1917 raids on London described the planes as "mobile magazines of death."

in political and military authority since the formation of David Lloyd George's coalition government late in 1916. Since he had taken no part in the jostling for power he was astonished to be called to London in late 1917 and offered the position of Chief of Staff of the Royal Air Force, which was to be born officially in April.

Trenchard accepted the post, but he had held it only a few months before he became disgusted with the political scheming of the Air Minister, Lord Rothermere, and resigned. His resignation had just been accepted when Rothermere himself became a casualty of intrigue and was replaced by Sir William Weir. Weir put Trenchard in command of an independent group of long-range bombers. It would be based in France, to put it within range of Germany, and its mission would be to strike directly at the enemy's factories. It would be the world's first air force organized exclusively for the purpose of strategic bombing.

The French objected. Any Allied force, they said, should be used to win the War where it was being fought—on the front. Again the classic air-power debate was joined. The airplane had proved itself effective on the battlefield, but the possibility of interfering with industrial production

On July 7, 1917, in the Little Britain section of London, firemen hose down smoldering rubble after the second air raid by German Gotha bombers—an attack, lasting 15 minutes, that resulted in some 250 British casualties.

and damaging civilian morale seemed remote to commanders who had the enemy in sight across a thin strip of no man's land. Trenchard compromised. The French let him operate on their soil without official recognition, and he made sure that his bombers hit plenty of tactical military targets in addition to their long-range strategic objectives.

More than half of Trenchard's airplanes were single-engined scouts that had to labor to lift 500 pounds of bombs and could not carry them far. He used these for nearby raids and saved his Handley Page 0/100 bombers for the long-distance runs into Germany. They carried nearly 2,000 pounds each and could fly for hours, though much of Germany was still beyond their reach. Planes that could have reached Berlin, the Handley Page 1/1500 and the Vickers Vimy, were under construction in England, but the War ended before either entered service.

Trenchard's casualties continued to run up to 50 per cent each month, half of them due to enemy action and half to accidents. On one awful day, July 31, 1918, twelve D.H.9s—new, longer range but unreliable de Havilland bombers just received at the front—took off to strike Mainz. Three went down with engine trouble, crash-landing near the trenches. As the rest continued toward their objective, they were attacked by 40 German fighters. The flight leader saw that they could not reach Mainz and swung toward Saarbrücken, which was closer. Four of his planes were shot down on the way. Five bombed Saarbrücken and turned toward home. Three more went down while they were still in German airspace. Two of the original 12 made it back.

Such heavy losses brought sharp criticism, but the Independent Force made the Germans pay a high price for the British casualties. Perhaps the most successful British raid was on the railway station at Thionville, where two direct hits set off a munitions train, hurling flaming shells in all directions and igniting several ammunition dumps. The fire wrecked buildings, destroyed five locomotives and 50 cars, then blew up another train.

There were 83 German military casualties in that raid, but usually the people killed and wounded by the Independent Air Force were civilians. When British bombers approached Düren, an unfortified German city that had never considered itself a target, bells were rung in warning. The people ran into the streets to learn what was wrong and were met with falling bombs. A raid on Bonn, where the people received no warning, killed 29 and wounded 60. A 1,650-pound bomb was dropped on Wiesbaden, whose contribution to Germany's war effort was not arms factories but hospitals caring for wounded men.

Thus the airplane gave the world a glimpse of total war, waged against cities, against civilians, against women and children. "An eye for an eye," a British minister had cried after the German bomb struck the Upper North Street School, and that is what the British exacted from Germany. Haig found such warfare repugnant, and disapproved of strategic bombing as a diversion from his war effort. But with his casualties at the front running more than 10,000 per day, and no relief in sight, even he could see no alternative to further strategic attack on the German nation.

The British raids killed 746 German civilians and injured 1,843, but RAF analysts later judged that the more significant effects were some weakening of the national will, a loss of production as people fled to air-raid shelters (the Badische chemical works at Mannheim, for example, were hit 15 times—but the air-raid alarm was sounded 256 times) and the diversion of combat squadrons and antiaircraft batteries to defend against the raids. A German officer agreed with the British analysis of the bombing. "The direct destructive effect," he said, "did not correspond with the resources expended. On the other hand, the indirect effect, falling off in production of war industries and also the breaking down of the moral resistance of the nation, cannot be too seriously estimated."

The German Gotha raids, which went on for a year, were fewer and less destructive than the British attacks, but they had similar effects. At one time the RAF had 400 aircraft standing by to defend against the Gothas—while Germany was using only 40 bombers. Germany, having lost more Gothas to accidents than to British defenses, canceled the flights late in 1918, believing they cost more than they were worth.

On November 10, Trenchard heard a rumor that a cease-fire had been arranged. All night he paced while his bombers pounded the Moselle Valley, and in the dawn, the rumor confirmed, he was at the field near the village of Autigny-la-Tour to watch every man and machine return safely from their last mission of the War. With typical dispatch he disbanded his headquarters and, on a mid-November morning, got in his car to head for home and presumably the twilight of his career. To his profound shock he found the village streets choked with British airmen who, on their own, had come to cheer him on his way. "I don't believe it," Trenchard muttered. "There must be some mistake."

He had written his Air Minister on Armistice Day asking to be put on half pay for a year, recommending that a younger officer be promoted to take his place, and expressing great weariness. "I am perfectly certain I am right in having a good long rest."

Lloyd George, returned to office as Prime Minister in the elections of December 1918, began the task of organizing a postwar government. Casually, in a note to Winston Churchill recruiting him for ministerial duties, the Prime Minister pronounced a death sentence on the Royal Air Force: "I am not going to keep it as a separate department."

But the execution of the RAF was stayed, partly because Lloyd George was busy preparing for the peace conference at Versailles, partly because the bungled demobilization of the armed forces led to massive unrest and riots that distracted government and military authorities, and also because Churchill, now Minister for War and the Air, did not intend to carry out the Prime Minister's wish if he could avoid it.

In February Churchill called Trenchard away from his "good long rest'' and asked for his recommendations for salvaging the Air Force. Trenchard immediately produced a two-page handwritten report proposing a tiny service with fewer than a dozen senior officers and two dozen squadrons, but with its own training facilities and above all its independence from the other services. Churchill compared this with the impractical recommendations of the Air Force Chief of Staff, Sir Frederick Sykes, for 154 squadrons at a cost of £75 million a year and immediately persuaded Trenchard to return to command of the RAF as its Chief of Staff while Sykes was sidetracked to civil aviation.

"I was left with nothing but two heaps of rubble," Trenchard wrote at the time, "one of bricks and mortar, the other of men. There were gems in each heap but I had to pick them out blindfolded." On all sides, political and military enemies tried to deny him the opportunity to succeed. Faced with impossibly large budget requests from all the services, Lloyd George imposed what came to be known as his "Ten Year Rule"—the military services should assume that there would be no war to fight for 10 years and reduce their scale of operations accordingly. Army and Navy spokesmen played to their penny-pinching audience in the government by suggesting that the Air Force be used simply to train pilots for their respective services. Trenchard never wavered in

In 1917 Queen Mary, escorted by General Trenchard (center foreground), inspects Bristol Fighters at the RFC field in St.-Omer, France. The royal review indicated air power's new status and was soon followed by the royal assent to the formation of an independent air force.

his determination to preserve the Air Force's independence. "I wanted very few squadrons," he wrote, "just enough to gain experience and carry out domestic roles in our overseas territories when local emergencies arose."

But Churchill had a tendency to "wobble when attacked," as Trenchard put it, and he wobbled now. It seemed to him much easier to let the RAF turn soldiers and sailors into airmen and to leave it forever in the shadow of the older services. Never one to conceal or contain his outrage, Trenchard stormed into Churchill's office to roar at the "absurdity of trained airmen becoming mere chauffeurs for the Army and Navy." After the shouting of both men died down, Churchill decided that this was the best argument he had yet heard, and he returned to battle on Trenchard's side. In October Churchill told the Cabinet: "The problem is not one of how many service squadrons we require, but one of making a sound framework on which to build."

Tenaciously, Trenchard preached his doctrine: "The air is one and indivisible," and the RAF must be regarded as "a force that will profoundly alter the strategy of the future." Churchill agreed and remained

The charred skeleton of a train at the Thionville station, in German-occupied France, is eerily silhouetted amid smoldering debris, a grisly testament to the success of a 1918 British bombing raid.

firm, and together they drafted a plan for the Royal Air Force that won approval first from the Prime Minister and the Cabinet, then from the House of Commons when it was presented as a White Paper. Little noticed at the time, it was a blueprint of the future of air power. The RAF would have three elements, the smaller two to work with the Army and Navy while "the main portion, the Independent Air Force, will grow larger and larger and become more and more the predominating factor in all types of warfare."

Approved in December of 1919, the White Paper lifted the RAF's death sentence but did not provide the money it needed to live. Trenchard asked for £15 million for the next year, and he proposed spending £13 million of that to build an RAF college at Cranwell. With the other two million pounds he would field only 25 and one-half squadrons— and of these, 19 would be posted overseas for a mission only he seems to have clearly envisioned, that of policing the Empire. The Army, the Navy and the budget cutters renewed their attempts to take back the ground Trenchard and Churchill had won and the issue was again in doubt until it was affected decisively by an East African leader known to the British popular press as "the Mad Mullah of Somaliland."

For 20 years the mullah—Mohammed Abdullah Hasan—had contested British dominion over Somaliland, and during World War I he had extended his control to half the country. By late 1919 the harassed British government faced the choice of abandoning the country or committing two divisions of troops and millions of pounds to a year-long campaign to rout the mullah from his network of stone fortresses.

Trenchard's reaction on being told of the problem was a bland question, "Why not leave the whole thing to us?" And in January of 1920 a dozen aircraft bombed and strafed the mullah and his supporters out of first one fort and then another, until, three weeks later, he was driven from the country with only four supporters at his side. At a cost of £77,000—the Colonial Under-Secretary called it "the cheapest war in history"—a three-week operation had succeeded where decades of combat costing millions of pounds had failed. Moreover, as Trenchard said in a speech a short time later, it had been conclusively demonstrated that air power could become an effective instrument of peace.

The lesson was not lost on the British political establishment, and while the challenges posed by a faltering economy, changes in government and the implacable opposition of the other services seldom slackened in the years to come, Trenchard got the money and authority to rebuild the RAF. For another 10 years he held his course, cementing his reputation as Father of the RAF (a title he said he despised) until in December 1929 he resigned, believing that he had been in command long enough and that it was time for younger men to assume responsibility. By then he had seen confirmed beyond dispute a statement he had made while preparing the campaign against the Mad Mullah: "An air force can't be built on dreams, but it can't live without them either and mine will be realized sooner than you think."

Curious Sudanese crowd a Khartoum airfield in 1919 to ogle a newly arrived symbol of British authority: an RAF Handley Page 0/400 bomber.

Policing the Empire from the air

Just after World War I, when disarmament threatened the Royal Air Force with extinction, Winston Churchill proposed a new duty for the young force: "Garrison the British Empire." Eager to justify its continued existence, the RAF briskly assumed its new role in 1920 by subduing rebels in British Somaliland with air attacks.

This new application of air power underwent a more stringent test in 1922 in Iraq, a British mandate riddled with violent dissension. The British technique there was almost quaint in light of later uses of air power in similar situations. On report of disturbances, RAF planes first dropped summonses calling the offending tribesmen to a court of law. If a summons went unheeded, the RAF returned, warning the locals with leaflets or loudspeakers that their village would be bombed on a given day and recommending evacuation. The bombing attacks usually were light, but they continued day after day until displaced villagers grew weary and complied with British demands.

Condemned by some critics as inhumane "bomb and scuttle" tactics, the Iraq raids in fact took relatively few lives. And they achieved their purpose: Eight RAF squadrons quickly quelled rebellion in Iraq, where 39 Army battalions had been hard pressed to maintain control. And here, as elsewhere, the RAF offered colonial authorities excellent communications where ground transportation was difficult and provided protection for British nationals in remote areas. Cheap, effective and relatively bloodless, aerial policing was soon extended throughout the Empire and gave the RAF a new lease on life.

In a supporting role under RAF command, armored cars patrolling a Middle Eastern desert follow signaled directions from an observer in a plane.

Loaded with bombs, a Vickers Vincent stands ready for a mission during uprisings in 1936. In policing actions, the RAF often strove for precision bombing that would concentrate hits on rebel leaders' homes, a practice that helped British airmen develop a high level of accuracy.

Used in what the British called sky-shouting, loudspeakers on the bottom of this Vickers Valentia bombarded colonial dissidents with threats.

Fleeing a rebellion in Afghanistan in the winter of 1928-1929, Europeans board an RAF Vickers Victoria in history's first major evacuation by airlift.

A lone RAF seaplane scouts the dramatic coast of Burma in 1929. The ease with which planes could patrol long stretches of rugged coastline and frontier gave them a great advantage over land forces.

A Vickers Valentia of No. 216 Squadron wings over Heliopolis, Egypt, in 1936. With a range of 800 miles, the Valentia could carry 22 troops and was used to move forces rapidly throughout the Middle East.

Supermarine Southamptons, the first flying boats of postwar design to be used by the RAF, rest at their moorings on a river near Baghdad in 1927.

RAF Hawker Harts cruise at 20,000 feet over the Himalayas in 1932. Several RAF squadrons were stationed in India, but insufficient funds and Army jealousy restricted the airmen to a subordinate role.

A bang-up show for the taxpaying public

"Aviation has never had such a day," exclaimed Britain's *Flight* magazine. "Never has it had such enthusiastic support from the public either." The occasion was the first Royal Air Force Pageant, on July 3, 1920, and the public's support was self-evident as some 40,000 people clogged the roads leading to Hendon aerodrome just north of London. Monumental traffic jams compelled many—among them Winston Churchill, then Minister for War and Air—to abandon their vehicles and walk.

The show proved worth the trek. Flying at altitudes politely calculated to avoid strain on spectators' necks, including some royal ones, RAF planes thundered overhead in awesomely complex formations, looped and rolled through aerobatics that left the sky a crazy tracery of smoke trails, lunged at each other in mock dogfights,

strafed and dive-bombed a network of trenches and sent a tethered balloon spiraling earthward in flames.

Originally conceived as a one-time event to raise money for the RAF Memorial Fund, the show was such a striking success that it was repeated annually for the next 17 years, drawing crowds as large as 150,000 and serving greater purposes than fund raising. It gave the RAF top brass a chance to evaluate the quality of pilot training and gained international renown as a showcase for new aircraft. And most importantly, the obvious popularity of the performances—particularly set-piece finales in which carefully planted ground explosives and smoke bombs discreetly assisted pilots in raids on mock enemy positions—convinced many politicians that the RAF was something taxpayers would not mind spending their money on.

At the first RAF Pageant in 1920, leading air officials (from left to right) Sir Frederick Sykes and his wife, Winston Churchill and Sir Hugh Trenchard share a private box.

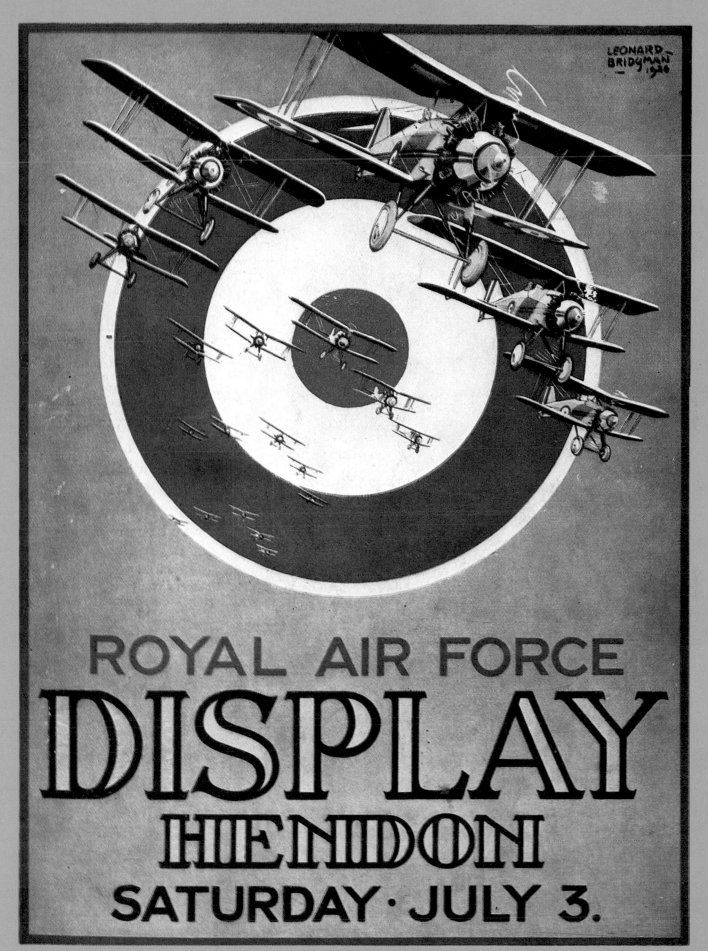

Gloucester Grebes zoom out of the RAF insignia on a 1926 poster. The show's name was changed to RAF Display in 1925.

Spectators climb atop their cars to watch Bristol fighters, Sopwith Snipes and Avro 504s line up for a relay race at the 1920 show.

King George V (left) endorses a Gloucester Gamecock fighter plane with a royal poke from his umbrella while reviewing new aircraft at the 1925 Hendon Display.

In crowd-pleasing displays of RAF precision formation flying, D.H.9 bombers simulate an enemy raid (right); two wedges of D.H.9s (bottom center and right in the picture below) converge upon each other; Hawker Furies (below, left) fly eight abreast with overlapping wing tips; and more Furies (left) pass low over a parked Vickers experimental bomber (foreground).

In the finale of the 1921 show, Bristol fighters swoop low to obliterate Scrappa Plain—a mock enemy village built partly of spare plane parts.

2
An explosive American's battle for bombers

One day in May 1917, at an inconvenient moment for the often short-tempered General Hugh Trenchard, a 37-year-old American major wearing an extravagantly tailored uniform appeared at Trenchard's headquarters in France. He was Billy Mitchell, the advance air-liaison officer for the American forces then gathering themselves to enter the War. With brash, easy assurance he told the British general that he wanted to see equipment, supplies, training, tactics and operations.

Trenchard's craggy face darkened. "One moment, Major," he snapped. "Do you suppose I've got nothing better to do than chaperon you and answer questions?" Mitchell used his immensely likable, boyish grin. "You've got a good organization here," he said. "It won't miss you if you take a day or two off." Trenchard's aide, Maurice Baring, well acquainted with his chief's explosive temperament, awaited the demolition of the impudent American. But Trenchard slowly smiled.

"Come along, young man," he said. "I can see you're the sort who usually gets what he wants." Trenchard spent three days introducing Mitchell to the air war on the Western Front. The two men became close friends as Mitchell quickly adopted Trenchard's basic ideas about air power: that the air force must be independent of frontline commanders, that it must pursue strategic as well as tactical objectives and that it must at all costs maintain the attack. These ideas would rule Mitchell's life and would lead him into conflict with senior military and political authority much like that faced by Trenchard in England, but with far more bitter results. "If he can only break his habit of trying to convert opponents by killing them," Trenchard said of Mitchell, "he'll go far."

On his arrival in France, Mitchell had borrowed space to set up an unauthorized aviation office, had spent his own money for supplies and travel, and then had asked Washington for $50,000 to fund his operations. His general replied that it was "not customary" to send so much money to a junior officer. ("It is not customary to have a world war," groused a member of Mitchell's staff.) Spending 10 days in the trenches, Mitchell became the first American soldier in World War I to see combat and the first to win the Croix de Guerre (awarded for the audacity of his

Radiating confidence in front of the Stars and Stripes, William "Billy" Mitchell shares the limelight with General John J. Pershing at a 1920 ceremony for Army fliers in Washington, D.C.

frontline activities). He flew over the lines with a French pilot and learned a profound lesson: "We could cross the lines in a few minutes in our airplane, whereas the armies had been locked in the struggle, immovable, powerless to advance, for three years."

He dashed off a long—and unrequested—report to Washington explaining how the Army should use aviation. He spelled out the kinds and numbers of planes needed, how they should be organized and how they should be deployed as an offensive weapon to seize command of the air. Only with that command established, he said, would ground forces be free to move. Washington's reaction was that he had not been in France long enough to become an expert. His report was ignored.

When Major General John J. Pershing arrived in France to command American forces in June 1917, Mitchell immediately proposed dividing the Air Service into two forces, one under the control of the ground commander to support combat troops, the other for "strategical operations against enemy aircraft and enemy matériel at a distance from the actual line." The latter force would have "an independent mission" and would be controlled by an Air Service commander.

The recommendation was far too advanced, both for a command that had hardly considered the use of air power and for the equipment available. At the start, as Henry H. "Hap" Arnold (then assistant director of the Army's Division of Military Aeronautics) later recalled, the Americans "had 55 airplanes, 51 of them obsolete, four obsolescent, and not one of them a combat type." Because of a mix-up in orders, the 1st Division set out for France in June without the Army's only air-combat unit, having left the 1st Aero Squadron at Nogales, Arizona. The squadron commander sent plaintive messages, but it was August before he and his planes got to France.

When the aviators arrived in France there was much confusion and an immediate squabble among their own commanders over how they should operate. General Pershing was disgusted. He thought his aviation officers were "a lot of good men, but they are running around in circles," and he called in a West Point classmate, a tough-minded brigadier general in the Corps of Engineers named Mason Patrick, to set them straight. But Pershing admired Mitchell's aggressive tactics and saw to it that he commanded the air-combat units at the front.

Pershing's headquarters, however, remained adamantly in favor of using airplanes to support ground troops. At critical periods, the headquarters staff itself selected aerial targets, and airmen were warned against harboring ideas of an independent force. Despite these restrictions, the Air Service gave a good account of itself in its two major engagements, at St. Mihiel and the Meuse-Argonne. Mitchell seized and held control of the air by massing enough aircraft—including some British and French units—both to serve the front's tactical needs and to pound the enemy's faltering air force on its bases behind the lines.

After Mitchell's success in France he was brevetted to the rank of general in 1918 at the age of 38. He became more flamboyant than

The special aura of a stylish airman

"He didn't walk like other men," remembered a pilot who had served under Billy Mitchell. "There was pride in every movement." Pride, flair, class, panache: Whichever word most accurately describes the visible, dashing quality that imparts a special magnetism to certain leaders, Mitchell had it.

It was in his dress that Mitchell's personal style was most readily apparent. "He was a plumed fellow," one reporter wrote wryly, "with the aura of banner, spear and shield." Mitchell even designed some of his own uniforms, adopting British touches such as patch pockets and the wide Sam Browne belt with its over-the-shoulder brace. These innovations set off a minor fashion craze among other American officers in France, but none could match Mitchell's unique and unmistakable style.

AS A CAPTAIN IN DRESS BLUE UNIFORM, 1915

IN FIELD DRESS, ABOUT 1918

WEARING FLYING TOGS OF HIS OWN DESIGN

IN FUR-LINED COLD-WEATHER FLYING SUIT

ever: He lived in a lodge once owned by King Louis XV, roared about in a racing Mercedes, rescued Eddie Rickenbacker from a chauffeur's job to put him into the air and personally spotted the last desperate German lunge across the Marne. His intense ambition did not interfere with his capacity for fun. He was ever the life of the party, a superb horseman, a crack polo player, a man who seemed full of the joy of living. There was something magnetic about him, his smile lighting his way, his body trim in a faultless uniform with row upon row of decorations.

A Chicago *Tribune* reporter described him: "Young, handsome and with the air of a conqueror, he personified war in much of its pristine grandeur. He flicked his boots with his handkerchief and committed many martial gestures annoying to confirmed civilians. No one ever had a better time being a general." When surrounded by Allied airmen, Arnold recalled, he practically held court as he talked enthusiastically about the air weapon. "The fliers around him would have done anything for him and so would the boys out in the squadrons." On the night of the Armistice in Paris, he had to be rescued from a joyful mob of French pilots cheering, *"Vive notre Général Américain!"*

His superiors, however, seem never to have shared Mitchell's conviction that he was destined for even higher command. In their eyes he was intelligent and prescient but more a quick study than an original thinker, broad but rarely profound. And he seemed utterly without ability to sense how others perceived him and the effect his behavior had on them. Thus when he most wanted to persuade his superiors he instead aroused intense emotional opposition that blinded everyone.

Billy Mitchell came naturally to a high opinion of himself. Born in December 1879—his parents were living in France at the time and he grew up speaking French as fluently as English—he was the grandson of a wealthy Milwaukee railroad baron and the son of a United States senator from Wisconsin. At 18 he abandoned college to fight in the Spanish-American War as the youngest lieutenant in the United States Army, shamelessly using his father's position to improve his assignments in Cuba and the Philippines. When he decided to enter the regular Army he wanted the Cavalry—but the Signal Corps offered quicker promotion to first lieutenant, so the Signal Corps it was.

It was a fortunate choice, for while Mitchell had a strong sense of tactics and strategy, he was also interested in applying new technology to warfare. Once, while snowbound in Alaska, he studied German engineer Otto Lilienthal's glider experiments, which had set the stage for powered flight. In a 1906 article Mitchell predicted that war would soon be fought in the air and under the sea. He studied telegraphy and photography, wrote a text on military communications and went on intelligence missions in Asia. In 1912, at the age of 32, he became the youngest officer ever chosen for the General Staff. Exultantly he wrote his mother, "I may be a general before many years have passed."

The post took him to Washington and he plunged readily into social life there and in New York. He added tennis to his sporting skills, rode to hounds in Virginia and entertained lavishly, running up awesome bills that he could pay only by drawing on his family's fortune.

As the only Signal Corps officer on the General Staff, Mitchell was drawn to aviation. The Army had been in no hurry to capitalize on the Wright brothers' invention, but in 1907 it had established the Aviation Section in the Signal Corps and in July 1909 it finally purchased an airplane from the Wrights. Lieutenant Benjamin Foulois took the airplane to Fort Sam Houston at San Antonio, Texas, and taught himself to fly with instructions and advice provided by the Wright brothers—by correspondence. In 1911 the Army bought five more airplanes, ordered Hap Arnold to learn to fly and the next year sent him to open the Aviation Section's flying school near Washington.

When Mitchell's tour of duty on the General Staff ended, he went to the Aviation Section as deputy commander and learned to fly. He and Arnold became close friends. There was a spirit of shared danger in the fledgling corps—12 of the first 48 pilots were killed before World War I—and a profound feeling that airmen were a special breed, unappreciated by the Army. With his enthusiasm, fierce energy and zest for command, Mitchell became their champion. Less than two years after joining them, dressed in a stylish uniform, he presented himself to General Trenchard and threw himself into the War.

The Armistice was signed before the new airplanes and strategic ideas could prove themselves, and Mitchell found a new mission to which he could apply his formidable energy and enthusiasm: convincing his country of the importance of air power. Arnold thought Mitchell should take over the Air Service. "Above all others," Arnold wrote later, Mitchell had "the background, the reputation, the personal courage, the knowledge of air operations, to do the job."

Mitchell agreed completely. He asked Arnold to line things up in Washington and soon was homeward bound. A Navy officer who saw him on board ship later reported that Mitchell was "fully prepared with evidence, plans, data, propaganda, posters and articles, to break things wide open." But the Army's indifference toward its upstart air arm soon became evident. An old-line infantry general, Charles C. Menoher, was named Chief of the Air Service and Mitchell became his assistant. Meanwhile American politics had become dominated by isolationism and a revulsion for war, and the military budget was cut and cut again. The Air Service received only a third of its requested appropriation and a report noted that "not a dollar is available for the purchase of new aircraft." For the next 10 years American air power would depend largely on dilapidated and dangerous planes left over from the War.

Still, Mitchell's enthusiasm was unquenchable. He organized a massive military coast-to-coast air race in 1919—the first of its kind—that demonstrated the potential of long-distance flight and contributed to the founding of a national system of airways and airports. His mind ranged far ahead of aviation developments and generated an endless series of

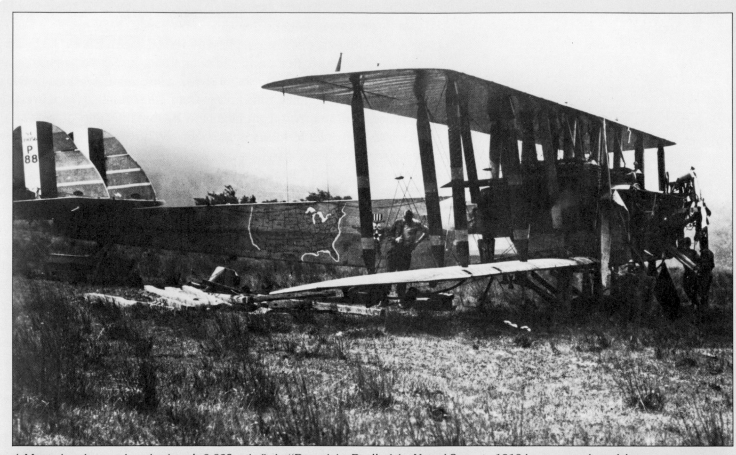

A Martin bomber used on the Army's 9,823-mile flight "Round the Rim" of the United States in 1919 bears an outline of the country.

Flushed with victory, Lieutenant Russell Maughan stands in the cockpit of his Army-subsidized Curtiss R-6 racer after winning the 1922 Pulitzer Trophy race near Detroit.

Army pilots gather around a globe before circumnavigating the world by air in 1924.

A push to conquer aerial frontiers

"The most necessary thing now," Billy Mitchell noted in 1919, "is to educate *the people* as to what may be expected in aeronautics and how it affects the well-being of every citizen of this country." As the No. 2 man in the United States Army Air Service, he plunged into the task, promoting many projects destined to make aviation a household word.

Mitchell organized the pioneering endurance flights that led to coast-to-coast airmail service. He encouraged Army designers to create planes that flew faster and higher than ever before. In 1924 one of his great dreams came true when two Army aircraft flew some 26,000 miles in 175 days to complete the first circumnavigation of the world by air.

Lieutenant John Macready, in high-altitude flight gear, stands next to his LaPere biplane before setting a 40,000-foot altitude record in 1921. Two years later he was one of two Army fliers to make the first nonstop flight across the United States.

proposals: aerial torpedoes, armor-piercing bombs, 37-mm. cannon for aircraft, a special corps of mechanics, air-raid protection for cities, air transports for hauling troops and paratroopers, expanded private aviation to provide a pilot pool for wartime, an all-metal bomber, aircraft that could take off and land on skis, amphibious planes, bombers capable of flying the Atlantic, and aircraft carriers with 900-foot decks.

Menoher, his reluctant chief, was exasperated by this outpouring. His reaction encouraged the airmen's feeling that their service was an unwanted stepchild of the Army. When Mitchell asked a General Staff officer what was being done with his recommendations, the man laughed and said, "We're filing 'em." The word went around the War Department that Mitchell's ideas were dumped in the basement on something called the "Flying Trash Pile." Arnold began to see changes in his friend: Mitchell became sharper and more alert but also more suspicious. An undertone of angry impatience became evident as Mitchell began to feel that he was being blocked by calculating enemies.

In response, Mitchell increasingly sought public support. A certified hero and a skilled orator, he was soon making frequent speeches and appearing regularly before Congressional committees. Gradually he clarified his message: first, that the airplane was the weapon of the future, and second, that the nature of the Air Service's mission demanded independence from the other services. Most military men were still oriented to the war just fought, he said, but most airmen were focusing on the next war, in which the airplane—especially the bomber—would dominate. The aims of a future war, he declared to spellbound audiences, would be to attack a nation's vital centers—its cities, factories and food supply—to break its willingness to carry on the war. He noted that in the past defending armies had protected those targets against attacking armies. But the airplane—his hand would shoot up dramatically, describing a high arc, as he made his point—would fly over the armies and attack the centers directly. As early as 1919, Mitchell was insisting that modern war engaged civilian men and women and children as well as soldiers. "The entire nation is, or should be, considered a combatant force." It was an argument Americans found horrifying.

The air force, he said, should consist of four groups. Fighters would seize command of the air. Bombers would attack vital centers. Armored planes—"flying tanks," Mitchell called them—would attack ground forces. And observation planes would continue to scout and direct artillery. Only the last two groups would support the ground forces tactically. The all-important first two, Mitchell argued, should not be controlled by ground commanders but should be organized along British lines as a strategic force, equal to the Army and Navy.

Airmen hoped that Pershing, who had organized the Air Service as a separate but tightly controlled component of the American Expeditionary Force in France, might support creation of a separate air force. But he dashed that hope early in 1920 when he said: "An air force, acting independently, can of its own account neither win a war at the present time nor, so far as we can tell, at any time in the future." He saw aviation as a branch of the Army, nothing more.

Mitchell refused to give up his campaign. His message and his personality were making him one of the best-known military men in America. Frenetically busy, he socialized, lobbied, wrote a book about air power and poured out articles, newspaper interviews, speeches and testimony. His points became increasingly oversimplified and his language more and more extreme, Arnold thought. In response, Mitchell's enemies focused on his personality instead of his ideas: A Navy officer, calling him "a politician in uniform," spoke for many when he said later, "We thought the cause was Billy Mitchell himself and not air power."

Fierce opposition came from three sides. Civilian authorities, geared to isolationism and Wilsonian peace policies, found his views on total war abhorrent and just the opposite of the pacific world role they envisioned for America. Army staff officers who once had considered him merely ridiculous now saw him as dangerous: When he said that future wars might be decided by airplanes before armies could even engage he was undermining an army already weakened by stringent budget cuts. And the Navy recognized Mitchell as its deadly enemy, for he had chosen the battleship as his demonstration target.

Mitchell understood that war-weary America was in no mood to support a policy based on attack, though no other role for air power made sense. He began to phrase his arguments in terms of defending against attack. The country's primary line of defense was guarded by the Navy's capital ships along the coasts—and now Mitchell declared that the day of the dreadnoughts was over. Airplanes could sink any ship afloat, he asserted, including the battleship. This was heresy to the Navy. The great battlewagons, the pride of the fleet, were considered invulnerable to anything but the heavy guns of another battleship. Mitchell went still further, deliberately challenging the Navy's vital interests, when he said that defense of the coasts should be turned over to the Air Service and offered Congress a complete plan for doing so.

"Good God!" Secretary of the Navy Josephus Daniels exploded, "This man should be writing dime novels." Daniels protested to the Secretary of War, demanding that Mitchell be silenced. He told a reporter he would be perfectly willing to stand bareheaded aboard any capital ship being bombed from the air, explaining that moving ships could not be hit. At that time the Navy had a small air arm, but the admirals were considering disbanding it. "I cannot conceive of any use that the fleet will ever have for aircraft," Admiral Charles Benson, the Chief of Naval Operations, said in 1920. On another occasion he observed, "Aviation is just a lot of noise." Naval aviators suffered as did Army aviators, but few were willing to join Mitchell's crusade for a separate service: They simply believed the fleet needed its own planes.

There were exceptions. A number of senior Naval officers did support Mitchell's position, even though they wanted the Navy to retain control of its own aircraft. One of them was the first chief of the Navy's Bureau of Aeronautics, Rear Admiral William A. Moffett *(pages 68-69)*. Another was Admiral William S. Sims, President of the Naval War College. "The average man suffers very severely from the pain of a new idea," he told Congress. He noted the new idea of a plane attacking a battleship and said: "The first position usually taken on such things is likely to be wrong." He thought the strongest defense against an attacking fleet would be an air force. Mitchell liked to point out that a thousand bombers could be bought for the price of one battleship. Sims said that he, too, would prefer "to put money into airplane carriers and the development of airplanes." And the respected naval theorist Admiral W. F. Fullam said in a widely reprinted article that in the future, "Sea power will be subordinated to or dependent upon air power."

Soon Mitchell issued a specific challenge. In an exchange with Representative Bascom Slemp of Big Stone Gap, Virginia, during hearings of the House Naval Affairs Committee in January of 1921, he said again that the biggest and best ships in the world were vulnerable to air attack. "It seems to me," said Congressman Slemp, "that the principal problem is to demonstrate the certainty of your conclusions."

Mitchell had been waiting for the opening: "Give us the warships to attack and come and watch it."

"How much money would you need for demonstration purposes?"

"We need no money," Mitchell said. "All we want are the targets and to have you watch it."

If his bombers could sink a great battleship, Mitchell was sure his case would be proved. "We are going to smoke these people out that do not believe in the air business and either make them fish or cut bait," he told a friend. To Arnold he said of the ships, "We're going to get them and we're going to sink them." The ships were available. Under the terms of the Versailles Peace Treaty, the United States Navy had acquired several German warships for experimental purposes—a submarine, a destroyer, a cruiser and a veteran battleship, the *Ostfriesland*—on condition that they be destroyed by August 1921. The admirals had planned to sink them with naval guns, analyzing each round's effects. These were the targets Mitchell wanted. The Navy resisted angrily.

The attitude was understandable, Mitchell told the Congressmen. "The trouble is that we do not like to see things destroyed that we have been brought up to revere and protect; that is human nature. The battleship is glorified. We think we can destroy it; it is our business to attack it and it is up to you to judge."

Mitchell was persuasive but the Navy did not give in until Senator William E. Borah of Idaho proposed cutting off shipbuilding funds until the issue was settled. Then the admirals reasoned that since no battleship could be sunk by aircraft, they would let Mitchell fail before the biggest possible audience. The ships had to be sunk in deep water under the terms of their transfer, and the Navy planned to anchor them on the 50-fathom line off the Virginia coast. Mitchell protested. His planes would have to cross 75 miles of open water with a heavy bomb load—

an unnecessary danger, he thought, since there was deep water closer to shore. But he finally agreed: "It was up to us to show that what we advocated could be done, so we had to accept the conditions as they were offered." He thought them "about as hard as could be drawn up."

At one point Mitchell was asked when the bombing could take place. Casually he answered, "Any time—tomorrow if you wish." That was sheer bluff; the Air Service had neither the planes, the bombs, the tactics nor the experience to do the job. He set a furious pace of study, planning and practice in January of 1921 to prepare for the test in July.

Mitchell organized the 1st Provisional Air Brigade at Langley Field, Virginia, with 250 aircraft and a thousand men. He structured it like a wartime strike force with fighters—pursuit planes, they were then called—and observation planes to support the bombers. Practice bombing began immediately on the outline of a 600-foot battleship laid out in nearby marshes.

The Martin Aircraft Company was building a big twin-engined bomber, the MB-11, that could lift more than 2,000 pounds, and Mitchell pressed for a May delivery date. Then he turned to the matter of bombs. The Army's biggest weighed 1,100 pounds—not big enough. He called in Captain C. H. M. Roberts, his ordnance specialist.

"Do we have a bomb that will sink a battleship?"

"No, we don't."

"Can you make one?"

"Yes, sir."

But there were problems, Roberts said. "First, we've got no money." He thought he would need $500,000, five times his annual budget. He would need authority to purchase materials without waiting for government purchase orders to be processed. And he would need a plane and a pilot at his disposal.

Though the General Staff protested, Chief of Ordnance General C. C. Williams gave Mitchell the emergency powers he needed to build the bombs at the Frankford Arsenal in Philadelphia. Roberts designed bombs weighing 2,000 and 4,000 pounds, bigger than any ever made before. He ordered seamless steel casings from a Pittsburgh plant that made torpedo tubes for the Navy. Steel noses, tails and fins were fitted to the casings. For the initial order of 2,000-pound bombs, a thousand pounds of TNT was melted and poured into each cylinder a bit at a time and cooled with a jury-rigged system using fans and ice water.

Roberts took the first bomb up in a Handley Page and—dangerously underestimating the weapon's power—dropped it from 2,000 feet at Aberdeen Proving Grounds. Later he recalled that "a pipeline straight to hell opened up below us, like a volcanic eruption. The plane was flung high in the air and the struts on the wings snapped all over the place." Now they knew, at least, that the bombs had tremendous destructive force—and that they had to drop them from a higher altitude.

The bombers would try to hit the ships to demonstrate their accuracy, but for actual destruction Mitchell was counting on the water-hammer

effect from below when the huge bombs exploded within 50 feet of a hull. The battleship—his most important target—had armor above the water line to ward off gunfire and watertight compartments below to minimize torpedo damage. But her bottom could be torn apart by the ferocious underwater shock waves engendered by a massive explosion nearby. This, at least, was the water-hammer theory, and all Mitchell's boasts, challenges and promises depended on its effectiveness.

Mitchell was determined to elicit the maximum possible public response to his demonstration. He assembled an aerial photography team, gave it 18 aircraft and said, "I want newsreels of those sinking ships in every theater in the country."

The pilots practiced bombing sunken hulks in Chesapeake Bay. They learned how to use the new radiotelephones installed in the bombers and rehearsed night bombing runs. When hazy conditions blurred the horizon, it was impossible to keep an aircraft level or to bomb accurate-

Planes and crewmen of Billy Mitchell's 1st Provisional Air Brigade line up on review at Langley Field near Hampton, Virginia, in May of 1921.

ly, so Mitchell got the Sperry Aircraft Company to develop the first artificial horizon; using a gyroscope, it displayed for the pilot the attitude of the plane in relation to the horizon. The men studied navigation, memorized the coastline, practiced sea rescue and developed their own meteorological service—tailoring all their efforts to the needs of the forthcoming bombing mission. As one officer put it, "Our men think bombs, talk bombs and expect to make the Navy eat bombs."

Mitchell's sole interest in the test was to sink the ships; the Navy's was in the details of the damage the bombs might cause. This divergence was evident in the rules the Navy drew up. The attacks would start with small bombs, building up to bigger ones on succeeding runs; after each run there would be a long delay while inspectors examined the damage. The Navy would be testing its aircraft in strafing and bombing runs alternating with the Army Air Service tests. Naval aviators had long sought the chance to show what they could do, and they were determined to make use of the opportunity.

On June 20, 1921, the naval transport U.S.S. *Henderson* left Washington with a group of notables aboard and the next day was in position to watch the first demonstration. The target was the *U-117,* a 207-foot-long German submarine that had torpedoed nine Allied ships during the War. Navy planes would strike first.

Mitchell flew out to observe in the *Osprey,* his two-place D.H.4b blue-and-white biplane with a long blue command pennant streaming aft. Mitchell had become a good pilot; several times he had saved himself and his passengers in skilled crash landings. And he knew engines; his mechanic said that Mitchell would hold a wing tip, order the engine run up and from the vibration detect errors in tuning.

With Mitchell wheeling overhead in the *Osprey,* Navy seaplanes flying at 1,000 feet straddled the target with 165-pound bombs and on the next run broke the U-boat's hull with direct hits. She went down in 16 minutes, "so quickly," a reporter wrote, "that it was hard to conceive

At Langley Field, Virginia, Army mechanics preparing for Mitchell's 1921 bombing demonstration unload a crated 1,100-pound bomb from a truck (above), place it on a trolley and roll it into a shallow pit (right). The Martin bomber was then moved over the pit so that the bomb could be fitted into a sling of steel cables under the fuselage.

that the trick really had been done." The civilians aboard the *Henderson* were impressed, but naval officers assured them that the sinking had no meaning. A submarine was merely a thin-skinned shell, they said; wait until the bombers met an armored warship.

On July 13 the flotilla, including the *Henderson* with its dignitaries, gathered around the *G-102,* a 312-foot destroyer built by Krupp in 1913. This time the Army had attack rights and Mitchell put on a show. Flights of pursuit planes raked the *G-102* with 25-pound bombs and machine-gun fire, a tactic designed to clear the decks of defenders. The pursuit planes were followed by the de Havillands with 100-pound bombs and finally by the Martins with 600-pound bombs. "They hit close in front of it," Mitchell wrote, referring to the ship, "behind it, opposite its side and directly in its center. Columns of water rose, smoke came out of its funnels and vapors along its decks. Then it broke completely in two in the middle and sank out of sight."

This time there was consternation among the naval observers on the *Henderson:* The ship had lasted only 19 minutes. But destroyers also were only shells, they maintained; nothing had been proved yet.

The armored light cruiser *Frankfurt,* built in 1915, buoyed with many watertight compartments, was the next target, on July 18. The first flights hit her with 100-pound bombs and did little damage. The next, with 300-pounders, caused only superficial deck damage. "Imagine that baby under steam and able to fight 'em off," a naval officer told a *New York Times* reporter. Another exulted, "I'm feeling safer all the time." Then the Martins struck with 600-pound bombs. One hit the water alongside the bow and the big ship heaved up in the water, rolling violently, and began to sink. At 4:48 p.m. the bow was awash; at 4:49 the mainmast snapped; at 4:50 she was gone.

The issue still was not settled, the naval officers contended. The planes had not yet encountered a battleship. The *Ostfriesland* would prove invincible to air attack. Built in 1911, displacing 27,000 tons, she had taken 18 direct hits and struck a mine at the Battle of Jutland and still had come home under her own power. There were no openings in her four-layered hull; her watertight compartments were not even pierced by telephone lines. "She was a wonderful ship," said the American naval officer who had brought her across the Atlantic.

On the day before the test, Mitchell flew out and spotted the *Ostfriesland* from a distance, huge, formidable, marked with red, white and blue target circles, awaiting the planes. He thought she was "like a grim old bulldog with the vicious scars of Jutland still on her. She was sullen and dark and we knew we had a tough nut to crack." Everything depended on sinking the *Ostfriesland.* The *Frankfurt,* the destroyer, the submarine would all be forgotten if Mitchell's fliers failed against the battleship. "We had to kill, lay out and bury this great ship," he wrote.

The next day the *Henderson* was crowded with top-ranking dignitaries: cabinet officers, senators and congressmen, generals and admirals, foreign observers from Britain, Italy and Japan. General Pershing

was there and so was Glenn Martin, anxious to see his new bombers in action. The fleet had come out, eight battleships, light and heavy cruisers, destroyers churning about sleek as greyhounds. They formed a huge ring around the silent German ship. The weather was foul, the wind gusting to 30 knots, beating the sea into whitecaps. The Navy decided that planes could not fly in such weather and postponed the test. Mitchell, furious, assured them that he was ready and ordered his bombers to take off anyway. It was a Navy trick, he thought: "In my opinion the Navy actually tried to prevent our sinking the *Ostfriesland*."

Naval planes were scheduled to make the first run, and hearing that Mitchell's aircraft were going to fly in spite of the weather, the Navy grudgingly ordered its pilots aloft. Their 250-pound bombs left the

While cameramen film the scene from hovering blimps, United States Navy vessels gather off Virginia for Mitchell's bombing demonstration. The six Army bombers overhead were preparing to attack the former German cruiser Frankfurt (second ship from left) at a signal from Mitchell's command plane, the Osprey (inset).

Ostfriesland almost unmarked. The Navy was right about the weather, a storm soon approached and Mitchell's Martins had time to make only one run with 600-pounders. They dropped five bombs and battered the ship's superstructure but did no obvious damage. "Naval officers sniggered cheerfully," a reporter noted, and one officer said that the odds were a thousand to one against the ship being sunk by bombing.

The next day offered perfect flying weather, bright and mild. But many of the observers, including General Pershing, had either tired of the rough seas the day before or had decided to wait ashore for word of Mitchell's expected failure. "I doubt if I shall waste more time on this croquet game tomorrow," snorted General Pershing. The Martins, carrying 1,100-pound bombs, were off at 7 o'clock and over the target at

12:26 p.m.   12:37 p.m.

8:23 a.m. The ship, slightly damaged by the previous day's efforts, had taken on a little water. She lay motionless, "immovable, as though she had been grown on a reef," a reporter said.

At 8:35 a.m. Lieutenant Clayton Bissell dropped the first 1,100-pounder and scored a direct hit on the *Ostfriesland's* foredeck. The Navy immediately signaled for the attack to stop so that the ship could be inspected, but she was hit twice more before the signal was obeyed. The control officer was furious, but that was nothing compared with the outrage of Bissell and his pilots at the cease-fire order. They could not land with the bombs they carried, so they dropped them into the sea— half a mile from a group of destroyers, "to give the boys something to think about." Even at that distance the water-hammer effect jolted the destroyers and they wheeled away. "They thought our crews had gone crazy," Bissell later reflected wryly.

The inspector found heavy damage aboard the *Ostfriesland* but ruled her still sound. "By Jove," said the commander of the Navy aircraft, "we're not going to sink this ship!"

At Langley the 2,000-pounders were loaded, one to each bomber. Then Mitchell got a new message from the Navy, ordering him to come out with no more than three of the big bombs. He was outraged. "This was the last straw," he said later. "We had an agreement with the Navy in writing that we would be allowed to make at least two direct hits on deck with our heaviest bombs."

Ignoring the latest restriction, Mitchell arrived over the target with seven bombers, each carrying a 2,000-pound bomb. At 12:18 p.m. on July 21, 1921, the first bomb was dropped. "It blazed in the sunshine as it tumbled over and over," reported *The New York Herald*, "landing 100 feet off the starboard bow. There was a muffled roar." From above,

The battleship Ostfriesland lists to port, rolls over and sinks in minutes after being struck by 2,000-pound Army bombs at the climax of Billy Mitchell's bombing demonstration. "It was," said Mitchell, "a very serious and awesome sight."

12:38 p.m.

12:39 p.m.

Mitchell saw that no flash of the TNT showed, indicating that the fuse had exploded it at the proper depth, 30 to 40 feet below the surface. "Under the green water the black smoke of the explosive mixed with white foam of the sea told us that a perfect detonation had taken place." He saw the battleship heel over 15 degrees and slowly right herself and he estimated that the bomb had moved 30,000 tons of water, more than the weight of the ship. The second bomb struck ahead of her and the third glanced off her starboard bow and exploded in the water, leaving a gaping hole in her hull.

At 12:26 the fourth bomb struck off the port beam and a minute later the fifth hit just 25 feet off the port side near the waist gun turret. The bow of the ship rose out of the water and the after turret, knocked askew, went out of sight as the stern began to sink. The ship righted herself but "rolled uneasily, plainly hurt," a reporter said. A naval officer sought to reassure him: "Pshaw! She'll float for days!" Water was still pouring from the *Ostfriesland's* decks when a sixth bomb lifted her stern. Now she listed sharply to port. Mitchell had one more bomb.

While naval observers continued to explain that ships with worse wounds had survived, the *Ostfriesland* listed farther to port, her bow rising sharply from the water. A huge hole was visible in her hull. The water line painted on her starboard side "crept higher as the hull climbed out of the water," the New York *World* reported. Finally, "she rolled there like some immense, round helpless sea animal. Her bow lifted still higher and her stern swung downward." She was sinking.

When her stern struck the bottom 300 feet below she held a moment, a hundred feet of bow out of the water, and then toppled forward. "It was as if the Washington Monument had been placed slantingly in the sea," the *New York Times* reporter wrote. Then the bow slipped slowly down and only a churning froth of bubbles and an oil slick remained. A Handley Page bomber dropped the seventh and final bomb in the center of the widening circle of debris—administering the *coup de grâce*. Twenty-one minutes had passed since the attack had begun.

The magnificent vessel's agony had made her seem alive, and left behind an overwhelming sense of shattered grandeur. Everyone was aware that an epoch had passed: A great ship had been sunk and the world's navies would never be the same. Aboard the *Henderson* many naval officers wept openly. The Chief of Army Ordnance said, ''A bomb has been fired today that will be heard around the world.''

The *Osprey* circled the *Henderson* at 200 feet. Mitchell doffed his helmet and goggles and everyone could see his grin as he waved to the applauding observers, and to all who had doubted the power of the airplane. Then he followed the bombers home for a wild celebration.

It was indeed a bombing ''heard around the world.'' The British air attaché wrote that the effect of the bombs alongside the ship was so powerful that ''it was immaterial whether these ships were possessed of 'watertight integrity,' '' a point that Trenchard used immediately in his continuing battles with British sea lords who insisted that near misses were total misses. In Italy, Douhet, on the eve of publishing *Command of The Air,* eagerly read the Italian attaché's report. And in Japan, where a thrust to become a world-class air power was under way, the reports and articles by Japanese observers were read with great attention.

Only at home was the prophet ignored. Amazingly, the United States military establishment refused to recognize the significance of Mitchell's bombing demonstration. He had supposed that if he could sink the ships his perception of air power would be proved correct and accepted. But the Navy acted almost as if the tests had not occurred. Much was made of Mitchell's using more bombs than ordered, and a joint Army-Navy board chaired by Pershing himself issued a judgment: Nothing conclusive had been proved about air power; the battleship was still ''the backbone of the fleet and the bulwark of the nation's defenses.''

Mitchell's own report was, of course, a complete contradiction of the board's findings; it included an argument for a separate air force. Although suppressed by his chief, General Menoher, Mitchell's report soon leaked to the public. A clash followed that led to the resignation of General Menoher and his replacement as Chief of the Air Service with that hardheaded engineer who had quelled the airmen during the War, General Mason Patrick. Mitchell promptly proposed a reorganization of the Air Service that would have put him in effective control. Patrick rejected the plan, saying, ''I propose to be chief in fact as well as name.'' Mitchell threatened to resign, and Patrick led him across the hall to the deputy chief of staff, who listened to an explanation and turned to Mitchell. ''Well, are you going to offer your resignation? If so it will be accepted at once.'' But Mitchell had thought it over. ''I don't care to resign,'' he said. ''I'll assist General Patrick along the lines he has laid down.'' It was one of the few times he ever backed down.

The man who gave wings to the Navy

Although most American admirals kept their faith in the supremacy of battleships even after Billy Mitchell's bombing demonstrations, the Navy had its own advocates of aviation—among them Rear Admiral William A. Moffett, who was named chief of the Navy's newly formed Bureau of Aeronautics in 1921.

Like Mitchell, Moffett was a forceful patriot who felt United States air power was dangerously underdeveloped. But while Mitchell wanted a single, independent air force, Moffett believed the Navy needed its own air arm flying from carriers. And their personalities contrasted sharply. ''Billy Mitchell was impatient; Billy Moffett was the soul of patience,'' wrote an admirer of Moffett. ''Mitchell tried to stir up a revolution; Moffett was trained in orderly development. Mitchell attacked personally all who disagreed with him; Moffett was a diplomat.''

Moffett's diplomacy eroded, however, in his dealings with Mitchell. ''We've got a fight on our hands to keep Mitchell from sinking the Navy, and the country with it,'' he said. They clashed head-on when the general tried to take the chair at a 1922 conference both were attending. ''Since when does a one-star brigadier rank a two-star admiral?'' Moffett demanded, and got Mitchell ousted from the conference. On another occasion he suggested to the press that Mitchell was ''suffering from delusions of grandeur or mental aberrations.''

But in his struggles with Navy leaders who resisted the development of a carrier force—''old fogies,'' he called them privately—Moffett eschewed argument in public, working tactfully toward his goal. His perseverance paid off in the late 1920s when the Navy began an ambitious program to build its carrier strength. By the time he died in a dirigible crash in 1933, he had earned the title the Father of U.S. Naval Aviation.

Rear Admiral William Moffett, tireless proponent of naval aviation, prepares for a flight in 1928. "Without an air force," he said, "the fleet would be a sitting duck."

Patrick turned out to be almost as ardent a supporter of the Air Service as was Mitchell, though always in ways consistent with the Army's ideas of propriety, and he did much to advance the cause of military and civil aviation in the United States. He learned to fly at the age of 60, the better to establish a rapport with his men.

Perhaps partly to remove Mitchell from the volatile Washington scene, Patrick sent him abroad to study air power. Mitchell, his formidable capacities as an intelligence officer engaged, toured Europe and produced a four-volume report weighing 10 pounds. Few in the War Department ever read the report, and no action was taken on it.

After visiting Japan to study its advances in aviation, and examining American defenses, he wrote a report in 1924, predicting with uncanny accuracy the attack on Pearl Harbor 17 years later that brought the United States into World War II. He predicted the day of the week, the time of day, the order of attack and the position of the enemy aircraft carriers. The official reaction, from the War Plans Division of the Army General Staff, was that "Many of the opinions expressed are based upon the author's exaggerated ideas of the powers and importance of air power, and are therefore unsound."

Mitchell, back in Washington by late 1924, was often summoned by Congressional committees, and his testimony hit harder and harder. He wrote a series of articles for *The Saturday Evening Post* that blasted military thinking. He was increasingly strident, and Hap Arnold pleaded with him: "Billy, take it easy. We need you. Air power is coming. Stop saying all these things about the independent air arm that are driving these old Army and Navy people crazy!" He remembered Mitchell's reply: "I'm doing it for the good of the Air Force, for the good of you fellows. I can afford to do it. You can't." His persistence cost him his position as Assistant Chief of the Air Service; when his term expired in early 1925 he was not reappointed. He dropped to his permanent rank of colonel and was sent to Fort Sam Houston in Texas as air officer.

In September a Navy flying boat trying a wildly impracticable flight from California to Honolulu went down at sea. And the Navy dirigible U.S.S. *Shenandoah* was sent over its commander's protests to brave Midwestern thunderstorms to fly over state fairs as a public-relations gesture. On September 3, 1925, a storm broke it to pieces, killing 14 men. The Secretary of the Navy reacted to the disasters by saying they proved aircraft could never successfully attack the United States.

Asked for a comment, Mitchell worked all night dictating a 6,000-word statement that he gave to reporters at 5 o'clock the next morning. It was a massive indictment of American military aviation and included this incendiary sentence: "These terrible accidents are the direct results of incompetency, criminal negligence and almost treasonable administration of the national defense by the War and Navy Departments." It seems evident that Mitchell intended to provoke a court-martial, and the noted American military writer S. L. A. Marshall later said that Mitchell had told him that in so many words. But it is less evident that he

intended to become a martyr. A man who knew him then observed that "he really expected to be hailed as a prophet."

The Army charged him with making public statements that were insubordinate and prejudicial to good order and discipline. He issued a press release a few days later that referred to "the barking of little dogs" and added that "It doesn't matter to me whether I'm in the Army or not." Clayton Bissell, who had led one attack on the *Ostfriesland,* recalled, "We quickly decided that Mitchell was guilty as charged. We even convinced him that he would be found guilty and we agreed that the trial had to be used to educate the American people on aviation."

Mitchell's defense was that what he had said was accurate. The trial began on October 28, lasted seven weeks and did indeed air his charges again, but as Mitchell argued the validity of what he had said, the Army tried him for saying it. The two sides talked past each other. Though there were reports later that one member of the court, General Douglas MacArthur, had voted for acquittal, the verdict was guilty—as expected. Mitchell was suspended from rank, command and duty for five years without pay. "The court is thus lenient because of the military record of the accused during the World War," the presiding officer said.

Mitchell resigned from the Army to continue his fight by writing articles and books. He was a national figure by this time, but the court-

Spectators queue up outside the Emory Building in Washington, D.C., for Mitchell's court-martial in 1925. The line went halfway around the block, but only about 100 people could fit into the courtroom.

Charged with insubordination, Mitchell stands to face the court as the indictment against him is read. At his table are defense attorneys, Mitchell's wife, Betty, her father and Mitchell's sister's husband.

martial finished him. He had nothing new to say and he grew more strident and less effective over the years. As the nation stumbled into economic depression it lost interest in the dangers and possibilities of air war and by the time Mitchell died in 1936 he was almost forgotten.

But by then his ideas had taken hold. His disciples in the Air Force had developed a doctrine of strategic bombing, and by 1935 had the aircraft, the Boeing B-17A, that could carry it out. The Navy, at least partly as a result of his challenge to its outmoded thinking about the invincibility of battleships, was developing a fleet of aircraft carriers. And in 1933 the Army Air Corps was officially given the mission Mitchell had volunteered to undertake years before—conducting land-based air operations in defense of the United States. His old adversaries were gone, and all over the world nations (including his own) were struggling to achieve the power in the air that he had said would be necessary.

During the court-martial, an angry general leaving the witness stand had burst out with an inadvertently brilliant summation of Billy Mitchell: "Mitchell is one of that damned kind of soldier who's wonderful in war and terrible in peace." And years later, his old friend Hap Arnold gave him an epitaph. "People have become so used to saying that Billy Mitchell was years ahead of his time," Arnold wrote, "that they sometimes forget that it is true." ～

Bombs that shattered
a ship and an era

The spectacular destruction of the battleship *Ostfriesland* by Army planes *(pages 62-68)* proved to an astounded public what later seemed a rather obvious conclusion—that nearly 25,000 pounds of high explosives dropped on and around a ship will surely sink it. But it proved no more than that. The big question was what to do next.

To Billy Mitchell and his eager pilots, sinking the *Ostfriesland* was just the beginning of what they wished to demonstrate; to conservative admirals in the Navy, it was more than enough. After several months of bickering, however, the Navy finally agreed to let Mitchell bomb the obsolete battleship *Alabama*, tethered in Chesapeake Bay, this time with a broad range of aerial weaponry.

The trial took place on a clear, bright day in September 1921. The first planes to arrive on the scene swooped in on the old dreadnought and laid a smoke screen to windward of her. This, coupled with a series of white phosphorus bombs that exploded on the ship's deck would blind any gunners in a dense cloud. "The saddest sight of my career," commented Admiral William Fullam, who watched with Mitchell from a nearby motor launch. "That takes all the fun out of the Navy." Tear gas and small demolition bombs followed with deadly accuracy.

That night the planes returned, and after lighting the scene with a star bomb exploded in the air over the ship, proceeded to strike its decks with 300-pounders. After three more days of bombing runs, Mitchell had a 2,000-pound blockbuster dropped in the water next to the *Alabama*. Her side torn open by the bomb's murderous concussion, she went under within 30 seconds.

A 1,000-pound bomb (left) and its 550-pound cousin are compared to the size of a man. Both sizes of bombs were dropped on the Alabama before she was sunk.

The Martin MB-2 bomber, a two-engined biplane, lumbers toward the Alabama with two 1,100-pound bombs tucked under its fuselage. The pilot and crew sat between the wings in an open cockpit.

An opaque screen of smoke laid by a low-flying bomber moves across Chesapeake Bay toward the Alabama.

A phosphorus bomb explodes on the front gun turret of the Alabama. Off her bow is the observers' motor launch.

The smoking tendrils of two simultaneously exploded phosphorus bombs splay out over the ocean as clouds of the thick gas cling to the battleship's deck.

A direct hit with a 300-pound demolition bomb sends a column of smoke towering over the ship's derrick-like masts.

Three observation vessels hug the side of the already-blasted battleship as inspectors go aboard to investigate the damage done by the aerial assault.

A team of observers stands amid the twisted wreckage of the Alabama's midships. The splinters in the foreground have been torn from the ship's wooden decks.

The effects of bombs on the ship's forward turret and deck are recorded by observers wearing gas masks as protection from lingering tear gas.

Proof of the vulnerability of dreadnoughts to aerial bombardment, the bridge of the Alabama is a shattered mess of twisted steel after Mitchell's preliminary bombings.

The coup de grâce, a 2,000-pound demolition bomb, explodes just to starboard of the Alabama with devastating results (inset).

Der Kämpfer im Luftschutz hat
so viel Verantwortung und so viel
Ehre wie jeder Soldat an der Front!

3
Secret genesis of a deadly force

The two men whom Adolf Hitler would later credit with building his World War II Luftwaffe found themselves, at the end of World War I, in strikingly similar situations, experiencing similar feelings of rage, humiliation and frustration. One of them was 25-year-old Captain Hermann Wilhelm Göring. On November 11, 1918, Göring leaned on the walking stick that the late Baron Manfred von Richthofen had used as a symbol of command and glared at the men of the Richthofen squadron, assembled by their Fokkers on a muddy field in northern France. He had a message from headquarters—the worst news Germany's most famous squadron had received since Richthofen had fallen in April and Göring, an outsider, had been named to succeed him. The War was over, they were beaten even though they did not feel beaten and they were ordered to fly their planes across the lines to surrender them to the French.

Göring was a magnificent pilot and a formidable fighting man who held Germany's highest decorations, the Iron Cross and the order Pour le Mérite, or the Blue Max, as it came to be called. He once said that when he was flying, "I feel like a little god." He acted like a little god now, declaring that he would ignore the contemptible orders and take the squadron back to Germany. When a frightened staff officer protested that such an action might jeopardize the entire Armistice, Göring reconsidered. He ordered five pilots to take their aircraft to the French but told them to crash-land the planes on arrival, to make sure the French would never be able to use them. He would lead the others back to Germany—to Darmstadt, well away from the Allied area of occupation.

The other man whom Hitler would praise as an architect of the Luftwaffe, Captain Erhard Milch, also commanded a fighter squadron, in Flanders, on the day the War ended, though he was not a pilot. He was almost a year older than Göring but had a round baby face with soft, nondescript features that were belied by his sharp and often very cold blue eyes. A man who knew him then said that when he spoke he barked, as if imitating an old-line Prussian officer.

On that last day Milch paraded his squadron for an exacting inspection at dawn, berated a hapless flight commander for insolence and held the men at rigid attention for 15 minutes. Then he gave them the ugly news, equipped their motor transport with machine guns and began the withdrawal to Germany. At the border he formed his men a last

A cold-eyed Hermann Göring, one of the prime builders of Germany's Luftwaffe, glares forth from a poster promoting the Air Defense League—a civil defense organization that helped to instill air-mindedness in the German public. "The air defenseman," reads the inscription, "is as valuable as the soldier at the front."

time to urge them to return home with their heads up and the Kaiser's colors flying proudly.

But the Kaiser had fled to Holland, hunger and unemployment were widespread, and Germany was erupting in revolution, with mobs of workers, Communists and anguished soldiers roaming the streets with red flags, attacking factories, beating officers and cowing police. The rioters in the industrial Rhineland reserved special rage for airmen, whom they held responsible for causing the War to be brought to their cities and the civilian population. Milch recorded his squadron's homecoming in his diary: "Into Germany. Not one of the swine welcomes us back—only the little children wave."

At about the same time, Göring was leading the remainder of the Richthofen squadron toward Darmstadt on their last flight. He landed first and at the end of the runway he deliberately ground-looped and destroyed his Fokker. A few days later, after they were mustered out, the pilots gathered at a restaurant to drink away their gloom. After a while Göring stepped onto a small bandstand, glass in hand. According to a man who was present, "There was something in his manner that made us all suddenly silent. He began to speak. He hardly raised his voice at all, but there was a strange quality to it, an emotional underbeat, that seemed to slip through the chinks in your flesh and reach right into your heart." Göring talked of the Richthofen squadron, its battles and its men lost. "Only in Germany is its name now dragged in the mud, its record forgotten, its officers jeered at," he said. Later that evening he had to fight off a thug who tried to snatch his medals from his uniform.

The next month Göring went to a political rally in Berlin in full dress uniform, captured the floor and cried: "I ask everyone here tonight to cherish a hatred, deep and abiding hatred, for these swine who have outraged the German people and our traditions. The day is coming when we will drive them out of Germany. Prepare for that day. Arm yourselves for that day. Work for that day!"

On January 10, 1920, the crushing Versailles Treaty clamped down on German life—its tight controls on German military strength, its suppression of German commerce and its ruinous schedule of reparation payments driving the country further toward despair. As the magnitude of the defeat and the harsh effects of the Treaty sank in, the German people became increasingly outraged, labeling the Treaty the Versailles Diktat and those who signed it the November criminals. The belief took hold that Germany had not been defeated but stabbed in the back.

In the months after the 1918 Armistice, the newly formed Weimar Republic had prepared exhaustive arguments and position papers for what the Germans thought would be a lengthy negotiation among equals at the Paris Peace Conference. Having stopped the fighting, rid themselves of the Kaiser and his imperial government, instituted representative government and blocked the Bolsheviks, the Germans actually expected the appreciative Allies to redefine, logically and honorably,

Grim-visaged General Hans von Seeckt, who toiled ceaselessly to rejuvenate the potency of the German military—particularly that of the air service—proudly wears at his throat the Pour le Mérite, evidence of his valor in World War I.

Germany's rightful place in the world. Instead, on May 7, 1919, the German delegates were summoned brusquely to the Palace of Versailles and handed a single copy of a 75,000-word document. Sign it within 15 days, they were told, or resume the fighting.

There was, of course, no alternative, but the German government agonized until the last minute before accepting the inevitable and signing. Then began the desperate search for a way to deal with the payment of reparations totaling some $130 billion (half the entire net worth of the country), the virtual dismantling of the German economy, and the reduction of German military power to a level of near-helplessness—including the utter destruction of the German Air Force.

Of the 440 articles of the Treaty, only five were required to dispose of the defeated nation's air power, so sweeping was their language and intent. Article 198, the first of them, made the intention plain: "The armed forces of Germany must not include any military or naval air forces." The next two articles ordered the demobilization of the Air Force and specified Allied rights to German airspace. Article 201 prohibited for six months (later this was extended to more than two years) "the manufacture and importation of aircraft, parts of aircraft, engines for aircraft and parts of engines for aircraft." And the last of the air articles dictated the surrender of "all military and naval aeronautical material" from complete aircraft down to components of aircraft instruments. Ultimately, the Allies seized or destroyed more than 14,000 German airplanes and 27,000 engines.

Germany descended further into chaos as 1920 began. In March a group of reactionary military officers occupied Berlin to replace the fledgling Weimar Republic with their own government, headed by a New York-born former official of the German Department of Agriculture, Wolfgang Kapp. He was declared Chancellor, paraded troops around Berlin and saw his attempted coup foiled by a general strike within 100 hours, whereupon he fled into exile. The Weimar Republicans returned to office, but during the disorder the militant Communist Party reappeared with renewed zeal, proclaiming its own notions of government, looting arms depots and ambushing Army patrols. One of Germany's most formidable pilots, Rudolf Berthold, was clubbed down as he led an infantry unit into the small town of Harburg and then was strangled with the ribbon that held his Blue Max at his throat.

The government seemed helpless to control the disorder until finally one man stepped forward and acted. He pulled together the Reichswehr—the tiny standing army that Germany was allowed to maintain under the terms of the Treaty. He suppressed the violence and imposed order, and began with implacable force and single-minded purpose to lay the foundations of a new German army and air force. He was General Hans von Seeckt, who in June of 1920, three months after the Kapp *Putsch,* was named chief of the Reichswehr.

A Prussian nobleman of high intelligence, Seeckt had joined his father's Grenadier Guards unit at 19. He became a member of the Third

Army general staff at the age of 31 and was a lieutenant colonel when the Great War began. Units under his command bloodied the French several times in the early months of the War before the entrenched stalemate set in, and he was responsible for some German successes on the Eastern Front in 1915. An erect, elegant patrician with a monocle often tucked in his left eye socket, he conversed fluently in French and English and discussed art and literature with the same ease with which he analyzed military strategy. He was 54 years old when he took command of the Army.

From the disaster of the trenches contrasted with the war of movement on the Russian Front, Seeckt had gained an unusually prescient view of how future wars would be fought: with relatively small but highly trained and well-equipped mobile armies, heavily mechanized and closely supported by aircraft. He envisioned, in short, the essence of what would later be called blitzkrieg, with its dependence on forward-striking aircraft. He foresaw what kind of army and what kind of air force Germany would need. And he knew that to get them he would have to begin building immediately, in secret, in direct and systematic violation of what Germany considered a cruel and punitive peace treaty. Years later he would admit that from the beginning he believed his mission was to "neutralize the poison in the disarmament clauses of the Treaty."

Even before he took command of the Reichswehr, Seeckt had acted to convert the innocuously titled Troop Office he commanded into a replacement for the Army's General Staff, which had been outlawed by the Treaty. And he ordered that 180 veteran pilots, chosen by the officers of the wartime Air Force, be placed in key military positions throughout Germany to keep up with developments in aviation. There they would remind the Army commanders of the role aviation would one day have in their operations and, above all, they would form the nucleus of the future air force that Seeckt was planning. Even at this early stage he recommended that the air force one day be established as a separate, independent organization.

Seeckt created a number of aviation sections in the Troop Office and staffed them with his best officers. These units were carefully concealed from the prying eyes of the Inter-Allied Control Commission that was trying to verify German compliance with the Treaty. Even as this was being done, in May of 1920, Seeckt issued an order required by the Treaty, disbanding the old Air Force. Drafted by the senior officer in the secret new air organization, Major Helmut Wilberg, the order dismissing the old organization concluded with a passage heavy with irony: "We shall not abandon the hope of one day seeing the flying corps come to life again. The fame engraved in the history of the German armed forces will never fade. It is not dead, its spirit lives on!"

Elsewhere in Germany, especially in the Rhön Mountains in the center of the country, the spirit of flying was being kept alive by another group of people, with different motives. Here young men led by former Army pilots who could not forget their love of aviation gathered to fly the one kind of aircraft that was overlooked by the drafters of the Versailles Treaty—the glider.

A member of this group, a former Gotha bomber pilot named Hermann Steiner—who wrote under the pseudonym Hauptmann Hermann—recalled how he and his fellow pilots in the War had felt "superior to the little beings down below, to the small business being enacted miles beneath us. We had a special sort of pride." Impoverished, often hungry, their only clothing old uniforms with the brass buttons cut off, the ex-pilots came together again on the Rhön Mountains in the summer of 1920. With bits of wood and scraps of cloth scrounged from the bleak leavings of war and revolution, they crafted gliders, laboriously dragged them up the mountains and launched them on downhill runs into brief, nostalgic flights. Steiner set an early record by staying aloft two minutes, but they soon discovered the secrets of soaring and were riding the updrafts for hours at a time. "This passion for flying," wrote Steiner, "which with many of us was almost a sickness, grew stronger and stronger during the next few years of revolution, inflation and unemployment, when life became all but hopeless and without point for great numbers of German people. For many of us, flying became the very meaning of life."

Among the spectators at the first Rhön meet was a former Army pilot named Captain Kurt Student. He inspected all the gliders and talked eagerly with the pilots. Soon a little financial assistance began to flow to the best of the glider builders, with admonitions to think in military terms. For the gregarious Captain Student was in fact the commanding officer of one of the secret air-force units, and his mission was to guide the love of flying into useful military channels. Years later, Steiner was incensed to find a monument erected on the gliders' favorite mountain bearing what he called a typical Nazi poem: "German nation, you must fly / And you will be victorious / Through yourself alone."

Said Steiner: "We young Germans who had traveled to the Rhön, starving and freezing, had done it without any idea of a war of revenge in the future. We had done it because we wanted to fly."

Just as there were two kinds of German glider enthusiasts—one interested in flying, the other in flying to war—so there were two kinds of aircraft builders looking for something to do in postwar Germany. Those who shared the ideals of the grand old man of German aviation, Professor Hugo Junkers, embraced the peaceful applications of flight and dreamed of building airliners, cargo planes, sports planes—of using aviation to improve the quality of life. Like Junkers, designers Hans Klemm, Heinrich Focke and Georg Wulf disdained to build warplanes unless they were forced to do so. But they had counterparts, including Ernst Heinkel, Adolf Rohrbach and Willy Messerschmitt, who would enthusiastically help Germany prepare for war. As the fliers would provide the manpower for the new air force, so the designers and builders would apply their genius to provide its machines. And in each category of effort there were some men who planned it that way and some who would not realize until much later what they had helped to create.

Despite the stringent efforts of the Allies, the Germans did not completely stop building new aircraft after the War. On the very day of the Armistice, November 11, 1918, Professor Junkers gathered his engineers and designers and told them to cease all military work and to concentrate on designing a civil transport. The resulting prototype, the F 13, took to the air three days before the Versailles Treaty was signed and rapidly became the most widely used transport aircraft in the world. The first orders for the enclosed-cabin, six-place, all-metal monoplanes were placed for the United States by General Billy Mitchell.

Junkers, the dean of German aviation, commanded the respect and fierce devotion of his employees and colleagues. Steiner, who met him in 1923, remembered him as a "little, wiry man" with a "miraculously youthful body, the important head covered with thick white hair, the large forehead, the blue eyes that sometimes seemed the eyes of a dreamer and sometimes the eyes of a cynic, the energetic chin—once you saw him you could not forget him." The War's horrors had made Junkers a pacifist. He believed that civil aviation was a way to link the nations of the world peacefully, an ideal that put him in direct and eventually tragic conflict with the direction his country was taking.

Ernst Heinkel suffered from no such conflict. A brilliant technician who thought only of warplanes, he was as delighted by the militant aims of the Reichswehr planners as Junkers was dismayed by them. Heinkel thought his career as an aircraft designer was over when the Versailles Treaty shut down the aircraft industry in Germany. Remembered as a physically and personally unattractive man—Steiner described him as "small, bald and fat, an unpleasant person to work with"—Heinkel had designed some excellent fighters and had pioneering ideas. In 1920 he was back in his hometown of Grunbach operating an electrical-appliance factory when he was approached on behalf of official American and Japanese customers interested in one of his wartime designs, a small floatplane that could be carried on a submarine. It would be a flagrant violation of the Treaty for a German company to build the plane, but that did not seem to bother the American and Japanese Navies. They put Heinkel back in business secretly, and he began filling their orders at his plant in Travemünde.

In 1922 the ban on German aircraft production was replaced by a set of definitions of certain civil airplanes, limited in size and performance, whose manufacture would be allowed. Heinkel was able to bring his operations into the open, although he still had to conceal the nature of the military aircraft he was constructing. Before long the ubiquitous Kurt Student, traveling under an assumed name, asked Heinkel to produce a hot little airplane that far exceeded the new restrictions. Heinkel went to work on what would become the HD 17, a reconnaissance biplane on which a single machine gun could be mounted. Then Japanese officers asked for a similar plane and for a torpedoplane.

Heinkel's life was getting complicated. The Control Commission

Professor Hugo Junkers (fourth from the right) is flanked by colleagues at an aviation exhibition in 1928. The Junkers W 33 Bremen—the first airplane to fly across the Atlantic Ocean from east to west—is on display behind the group.

charged with enforcing the Treaty made unannounced inspections to search for violations, and Heinkel was at a loss for a way to conceal so many kinds of military aircraft. The problem was solved by his Japanese customers. Japan's naval attaché in Berlin was a member of the Commission; when a surprise inspection of Heinkel's plant was scheduled, the attaché would let him know in advance. Thus, Heinkel said later, "an extremely risky game of hide and seek began, and I am bound to admit that it appealed to a man who was given to taking risks." The system worked and he was never caught.

Soon other German aircraft manufacturers were operating, both in and out of Germany. Claudius Dornier first opened factories in Switzerland and Italy to avoid the Treaty provisions and then reopened in Germany, where he produced a flying boat. Heinrich Focke and Georg Wulf founded Focke-Wulf in 1924. Willy Messerschmitt took over the Bavarian Aircraft Company and—always with future fighters in mind—started building high-speed sports aircraft. Adolf Rohrbach, producing all-metal flying boats in Berlin and Copenhagen after 1922, developed the smooth metal stressed skin with flush rivets that would become standard for the world's aircraft. On one occasion a Control Commission inspection team arrived without warning when a new Rohrbach bomber was standing in the hangar. While the plant manager stalled, workers piled ladders, dust covers and assorted equipment against the new plane. The inspectors walked past without noticing it.

Thus, within a few years of the end of the War, General von Seeckt's new air force was germinating. His aviation officers had reached out to the civilian builders and fliers, had studied what other countries were doing, and were making their plans. But a pilot is not made by planning: He must fly. Private flying clubs had begun to blossom, and the military began using them to train pilots. But a military pilot must fly warplanes in simulated combat, impossible in the closely watched Germany of the 1920s. For that kind of training, and for production of combat aircraft, Seeckt looked to Russia.

Germany and Russia were essentially still enemies, but both were prostrate—Germany from defeat, Russia from revolution and civil war—and for the moment each needed the other. Seeckt courted the proletariat dictators to the east, and an era of covert military cooperation began with the 1922 Treaty of Rapallo, which ended reparations payments and formalized several trade agreements. Seeckt's emissaries had already called on Professor Junkers with a proposition: He would be paid a secret subsidy to erect a new plant at Fili, near Moscow, to make warplanes. The old professor resisted, but when the Army also promised him airline rights in Russia, he gave in. As distasteful as the military applications of aviation were to him, he steadfastly believed that

Inside the Junkers secret aircraft factory at Fili, near Moscow, German technicians assemble around the partly completed wing of a plane. A row of large C clamps holds the corrugated metal skin fast to the underside of the wing.

airlines, by acquainting the peoples of the world with one another, could promote understanding and peace.

Soon the Germans struck a new deal with the Soviet Union. In return for training Soviet army and air force personnel, Germany was allowed to open its own highly secret military flight center at Lipetsk, 220 miles from Moscow. "Around two runways," an officer wrote, "there came into being a large complex of hangars, loading docks, production and repair shops." By 1926 the field was fully operational as a training and aircraft-testing center, disguised as a Soviet base. During the next eight years about 120 young German fliers would be turned into excellent military pilots, skilled in bombing and aerial combat. While relatively few, these men were sufficient to form the nucleus of the air force.

All this was done under tight secrecy. The men received their mail through a Berlin box number and their supplies in unmarked boxes that followed circuitous routes. Aircraft were flown in at night at very high altitudes. When airmen were killed in accidents, their bodies were sent home in boxes labeled as machine parts. Fliers whose tours were over came back to Germany on Soviet ships out of Leningrad and were landed on lonely shores at night.

Covert military activity provided an essential base and an invaluable cadre with which to build German air power, but the greatest gains were made in the open, by the civilian airlines. Immediately after the War,

New planes stand on the bleak, snow-clogged runway of the Fili plant. At left is a Ju F 13—the world's first all-metal transport aircraft. The other two airplanes are small Junkers trainers used to instruct novice Soviet and German fliers.

airlines sprang up all over Germany; 38 were operating by 1924. Some were haphazard operations consisting of one pilot flying a war-surplus airplane, but they did constitute flying activity, and they did not escape the notice of General von Seeckt and his colleagues. In 1924 the government created the Ministry of Transport, with a civil-aviation department—and Seeckt hand-picked the man to head that department, Captain Ernst Brandenburg. Brandenburg understood the military significance of a vigorous air-transport industry, and he moved decisively.

To consolidate the fragmented industry Brandenburg withheld government subsidies—the lifeblood of the fledgling airlines—from all but two companies: Junkers Airways and Deutscher Aero Lloyd. All of the others soon folded, but Brandenburg was still not content. He wanted all German air transport abroad controlled by the state. In contrast, Professor Junkers was putting together route combinations that would knit Europe into a tight network of pacific, open, international cooperation. Brandenburg made his dissatisfaction public when he said in a speech that the government could hardly support a course that, if continued, "will be marked by later historians as the first outstanding step on the road to the United States of Europe."

The government had a weapon to use against Junkers. The old professor had poured his capital into the plant at Fili, depending on the government's promise to reimburse him. Now the government claimed his company had inflated its accounting of the losses incurred at Fili to increase the subsidy, and it refused to make final payment unless he turned his airline over to the state. Financially hard pressed, Junkers finally agreed, and in 1926 his company and Aero Lloyd were combined to form Deutsche Luft Hansa Aktiengesellschaft—German Air Union Incorporated.

Another piece of the military planners' grand design fell into place when the government named Erhard Milch, then a 33-year-old Junkers executive, as one of the new airline's three directors. Loyal Junkers employees resented Milch's profiting from the idealistic old man's loss and could not understand why a second-echelon manager had been selected. They had known Milch as a friendless loner and were not aware that for some time he had been quietly cooperating with Seeckt's air-force planners.

Seeckt's own position was eroding badly. His Prussian arrogance and his open contempt for the politicians in Berlin did not endear him to the Social Democrats who were busy remaking Germany. He became embroiled in ever more numerous and more dangerous squabbles. When Seeckt offered the Kaiser's grandson, Prince Wilhelm of Prussia, a military post, the resulting storm of protest from anti-Royalists led to Seeckt's resignation. The loss of Seeckt's unstinting faith in the future German air force would be felt. But the foundations he had set were firm, and the men he had caused to be put in place—most conspicuously Erhard Milch—went on without pause to the next phase of the rebirth of German air power.

After the War Erhard Milch had served with a police air squadron until 1921, when he joined the Junkers airline. He was manager of the airline's Berlin-Danzig mail route when the F 13s were introduced. In May 1921 the Allies had noticed the obvious—that the manufacture of the F 13s violated the peace treaty—and threatened to occupy the Ruhr unless the production of offending aircraft was stopped. Existing aircraft were ordered surrendered to the Allies.

The German government promptly promised to comply, but Erhard Milch did not. The Control Commission ordered the planes confiscated, but it identified them only by registration number. Milch soon had men with paintbrushes changing registration numbers faster than the Control Commission could account for them. A French officer leading one search scratched at the number on an F 13 and exclaimed that there was another number underneath. "Keep scratching," said Milch, in a cool display of his contempt. "You will find a lot more." The Control Commission cracked down and in October of 1921 forced a seven-month suspension of Junkers airline operations on the Danzig route.

Milch was soon promoted to Junkers' headquarters at Dessau, where Captain Steiner, then a Junkers official, remembered him as a man who "always seemed alone." In 1924 he went to Buenos Aires to establish a Junkers subsidiary airline in South America. He made a visit to the United States and, after seeing Henry Ford's revolutionary assembly line, came to understand the vast dimensions of American industrial power.

It was à year after Milch's return from his trip to America that Brandenburg named him one of the directors of Luft Hansa. It immediately became apparent that Milch understood where the real future of German aviation lay, that he was in close touch with Seeckt's planners, and that he was the real leader of Luft Hansa.

First of all, Milch set out to put Luft Hansa on a sound business footing. He was an excellent manager with a grasp of finances and a mind for technical detail. It was a good combination and this clearly was the happiest period of his life. Luft Hansa flew 93,000 passengers in its first year, averaging 25,000 miles a day. In its second year it nearly doubled the mileage figure. Routes were extended from Germany to England, through Italy and Portugal to Africa, through Moscow to Peking. On seeing two great Junkers planes passing overhead, a German woman wrote home from China: "There I stood, gazing as they flew like enormous birds toward the lilac-colored mountains in the west. I scarcely noticed the tears running down my cheeks. This was Germany calling and beckoning us from the Fatherland."

Milch sent a Dornier Do 15 Wal flying boat to investigate a route to Brazil. In South America the Kondor Syndikat, an offshoot of Luft Hansa, began extending its routes along the Brazilian coast and soon had linked up with a German-operated line in Colombia. Milch arranged to equip the transatlantic passenger liners *Bremen* and *Europa* with catapults and seaplanes. When the ships were still several hundred miles from port, the planes were launched to carry the mail the rest of the way, thus reducing by a day or more the time needed to get the mail across the ocean.

But the military planners with whom Milch was working were interested most of all in training pilots, and Luft Hansa soon had six full-fledged paramilitary training schools in operation, each turning out a hundred pilots a year. At the same time Milch was pushing for the invention and production of better equipment, including instruments for blind flying, and insisting on the most advanced training for pilots. Steadily, Milch developed for Luft Hansa what the military fliers needed but were prevented from obtaining themselves: improved navigation training, beacon-lighted airways and ground-control radio stations.

Gradually the Allies wearied of enforcing the fine points of the Versailles Treaty. That weariness was enhanced by Captain Brandenburg's Civil Aviation Department, which vigorously enforced a fine point the Allies soon wished they had not put in the Treaty. It required that non-German planes operating in the country observe the same restrictions as those that were imposed on German aircraft. Thus the Allies' own rapidly developing airlines were severely limited in the aircraft they could fly to Germany, and they began exerting pressure on their governments to ease the rules. On May 21, 1926, a new concord, the Paris Air Agreement, removed all the technical restrictions on production of German civil aircraft. The restrictions on military aviation remained in effect, but the Control Commission was abolished in 1927, and thereafter the German aviation industry was virtually free of foreign interference—as long as it did nothing so flagrant that the Allies would have to bestir themselves.

Soon Heinkel's firm was manufacturing fighters and torpedo planes, Messerschmitt was building the forerunners of his great fighters and Dornier was producing giant flying boats. From the premier designer, Professor Junkers, came three-engined transports that evolved into the highly successful Ju 52. At least a dozen warplanes were tested at Germany's secret Russian base at Lipetsk.

All of this activity had to be concealed not only from the Allies but also from powerful forces in the German government that hoped they could get some of the harshest conditions of the Versailles Treaty changed by rigorously abiding by its terms. "The period was full of intrigues," Captain Steiner said later. "Many murders were committed with the sole purpose of keeping secrets."

Milch, meanwhile, had managed to make himself as unpopular at Luft Hansa as he had been at Junkers. When he went on a test flight in an experimental aircraft, his own deputy exclaimed aloud, "I hope it crashes." There were also political attacks from those who resented the large government subsidies to Luft Hansa. Late in the decade a liberal coalition in the Reichstag—led by three deputies being paid by Junkers loyalists—managed temporarily to cut the subsidies. In response, Milch began buying the services of a few deputies of his own, one of them a

Sport flying for war

When German leaders decided to secretly develop the country's air power despite the prohibitions of the Versailles Treaty, they found a ready-made foundation for their ambitious project in the German people's long-standing love of flying for sport.

The oldest German flying club was the Deutschen Luftsport Verband (German Sport Aviation Association), founded by gliding enthusiasts in 1902. Luftsport Verband had languished during World War I but was revived in 1920 and, with government encouragement, precipitated a gliding craze that swept the country.

In 1924, after the Allies let Germany have a few powered aircraft for sport flying, aviators started a new club, Sportflug G.m.b.H. (Sport Flying Limited) and began training private pilots.

The government invested heavily in both civilian associations. By 1925, with 10 Sportflug pilot-training centers in operation and 50,000 people enrolled in aviation societies, fully half the Reichswehr's $2.5-million aviation budget was being used to subsidize civilian clubs.

By 1935, the Luftwaffe had emerged as a world air power, but Hitler's Nazi government, by such means as the posters shown here, was still vigorously promoting civilian aviation as a continuing source of support and manpower for Germany's growing air force.

Posters of the mid-1930s urge people of all ages to "Join the German Sport Aviation Association." They depict Hitler Youth who built and flew model aircraft for rich government prizes (top left), the splendor of a flight over the Rhine (top right), and closer to the real aims of the Third Reich, paramilitary formation flying (bottom).

recently elected Nazi whose flaming Right-Wing rhetoric and imposing presence appealed to Milch. His name was Hermann Göring.

After spending the postwar years selling parachutes, flying charter aircraft and touring as an exhibition flier in Sweden, Göring had returned to his home in Munich in 1921. There he had been attracted to Adolf Hitler's new National Socialist German Workers' Party, which virulently opposed abiding by the Versailles Treaty and maintained an 11,000-man army of brown-shirted Nazi thugs—the Sturmabteilung (Storm Detachment), or SA—that battled Leftists in the streets. Hitler welcomed the respectability conferred on the party by Göring's fame as a war hero. Appointed commander of the SA, Göring whipped the organization into a disciplined and effective force and soon became second only to Hitler in the Nazi power structure.

Thus Göring was at Hitler's side in November of 1923 when the Nazi leader took over a Munich beer-hall rally at gunpoint and announced his intention to seize the Bavarian government. A few hours later, marching through cheering crowds to occupy the government buildings, the Nazis were met and fired on by a loyal police force. Hitler injured a shoulder as he dived to the ground. Göring took a bullet in the thigh. Hitler was arrested and sentenced to prison, where he worked on

A party of Pimpfe—boys in the lowest rank of Hitler Youth—take turns launching fragile handmade model gliders near Berlin in 1935. The government encouraged this hobby to maintain air-mindedness while most flying activities were forbidden in Germany after World War I.

his manifesto for Germany, *Mein Kampf;* Göring went into exile in Sweden. His gunshot wound became infected and he lived in constant pain that led to an addiction to morphine for which he was twice committed to mental hospitals. He finally overcame his addiction, but some of his associates thought he was never the same afterward.

Göring returned to Germany under a political amnesty in 1927 as Hitler, released from jail, was busy rebuilding the Nazi Party. Despite his wound and prior service to the party, Göring found that he had to win his way back into Hitler's confidence by astute politicking—both inside the party and on behalf of the party—and in doing so assumed a fawning attitude toward Hitler that he never lost.

Göring played no part in German aviation or the secret growth of air power until 1928, when he was elected to the Reichstag as one of 12 Nazi deputies. His chief role in the party was to bridge the gap between the thugs in the SA, who were fighting bloody battles with Communist street armies, and the financial and industrial leaders whose support Hitler needed in his drive to take over the German government. Göring spoke the language of both groups.

In 1930 the Nazi Party won 108 seats in the Reichstag and became for the first time a serious factor in German politics. Göring, by then the

A group of one-man gliders takes off from a hillside at Trebbin near Berlin while a crowd of admiring spectators watches. Teams of jack-booted Brownshirts pulled the gliders into the air with long wire cables, which were slipped loose by the pilots once their craft were aloft.

party's political director and chief spokesman, soon was elected President of the Reichstag. The German government, battered by world-wide depression and the effects of the reparations payments, whip-sawed by the violent street battles between Left and Right, was having ever-greater difficulty in governing.

During the 1932 election campaign, Milch quietly permitted Hitler the free use of a Luft Hansa airliner for his speechmaking tours. The Nazis took 37 per cent of the vote and won 230 seats in the Reichstag. Although they held fewer than half the 608 seats, they now constituted the Reichstag's largest delegation. The government was being squeezed to death. Late in 1932 there was another election and in January of 1933 still another. At the end of January Hitler, having put together a coalition that gave him the balance of power, was made Chancellor.

Göring was named to several jobs in the new government, including commissioner of civilian aviation, and although the Ministry of Defense tried to maintain its control of military aviation, it was hopelessly and quickly outmaneuvered by the veteran Nazi intriguer. Just a few months later Göring was appointed chief of a new Air Ministry, with authority over both military and civilian aviation. In August he was given the rank of general, and with it the authority and the prestige he wanted to put himself conspicuously at the head of a strong and independent air force.

Even before the change in government came about, Göring had been trying to recruit Erhard Milch to be the future Secretary of State for Air—the Air Ministry's executive officer. Milch was reluctant to leave his beloved Luft Hansa, but after several meetings with Hitler, including one in which the Nazi leader discussed at length the theories of the Italian General Douhet, Milch became convinced that Germany needed Hitler's leadership. "In the air we shall of course be supreme," Hitler had said before his accession to power. "It is a manly weapon, a Germanic art of battle; I shall build the largest air fleet in the world." And when Hitler told Milch, "Germany needs you in this office," the latter accepted his new position and the rank of general that came with it.

Professional military men sneered. "Milch may be an able general manager," said one officer, "but he will never be a general." There was also the troublesome fact that Milch's father was a Jew, and Hitler, in his fanatical hatred of Jews, was intent on removing them from German society. Milch solved this problem by prevailing on his aging mother to execute an affidavit that said Milch was not the son of her Jewish husband but the product of an adulterous affair with a racially pure German. After that, behind his back, Nazis referred to Milch as the "honorary" Aryan.

The relationship between Milch and Göring was neither close nor consistent. When Hitler said in a speech, "Two names are ineradicably linked with the birth of our Luftwaffe—Göring and Milch," it was the last straw for the jealous Göring, who by then considered Milch a rival. He encouraged Milch's many enemies and spoke with disparaging vul-

"Dummy Bombshell, Danger!" reads a sign being set in place by a soldier before one of the many mock air raids staged in Berlin in the years preceding World War II.

A Berlin woman is helped from an air-raid shelter after a simulated poison-gas attack, during which planes showered the streets with harmless chemicals.

garity of Milch's supposed reluctance to expand the air force as fast as Göring wanted to, saying, "I kick him in the ass and he multiplies the front line in a matter of weeks." When the harassed Milch asked to be returned to Luft Hansa, Göring refused, warning his deputy not to feign illness to get away—though suicide would be acceptable.

As uneasy as their relationship was, Milch was indispensable to Göring as a powerful and effective organizer who understood Hitler's intention to make the air force the keystone of Germany's strength and the cutting edge of an aggressive foreign policy. To accomplish this would require even more flagrant violations of the Versailles Treaty— violations that could not be hidden for long.

Milch tried to convince the watching Allies and German pacifists that Germany needed strength to defend itself against airborne aggression. In June 1933, Berlin newspapers announced that unidentified aircraft had dropped leaflets on the city. No evidence was ever produced to support the allegations, but Milch told reporters, "Such leaflet attacks demonstrate that our very existence is threatened." One newspaper said in an editorial, "Germany, with clipped wings, pulled claws, must sit idly by while its nest is befouled." "Today it is only leaflets," warned another, "but tomorrow it will be bombs." Two days later a civil-defense organization called the Federal Air Protection League started erecting big dummy bombs all over Berlin as grim reminders, established air-raid districts, built shelters, appointed wardens and held drills. These activities focused attention on the possibilities of enemy bombing and the inability of Germany to defend itself in the air.

After Göring had succeeded in gaining complete control over the air force, he left the running of it to Milch. Göring was at the same time involved in economic development, internal affairs and the creation of a police state. He organized the precursor of the Gestapo, established concentration camps and began filling them with opponents of the Nazis, opened dossiers on his enemies, established spy systems throughout the society and began the systematic persecution of Jews. Göring found murder an acceptable political technique, but when casual torture and sexual abuse became common in the camps he began to protest. The Nazi hierarchy sneered at his squeamishness and in the spring of 1934 turned the police, Gestapo and the camps over to Heinrich Himmler.

Göring preferred the genteel life. He became an unrestrained bon vivant who loved his frequent and famous parties. He stuffed himself with rich foods and soon fattened to 280 pounds. He used his power to line his own pockets and developed a taste for elaborate uniforms, ostentatious medals, jewels, fine paintings and country homes, including an opulent hunting lodge named Karinhall. And he continued to seem genial, reasonable and reassuring when most of his confederates sounded like wild men. Years later Göring's wife Emmy quoted the British Ambassador, Sir Nevile Henderson, as saying, while the world was slipping toward war, "I wish I had not to deal with anybody in

Germany except your husband. One can talk so openly with him. He always remains calm, intelligent and logical."

With Hitler in charge of the government, Göring in command of aviation and Milch firmly in control of planning, German aviation after 1933 became a booming industry. The air budget soared far beyond the amount that was publicly admitted. Milch broke ground for a huge new Air Ministry headquarters that was designed to symbolize the importance of air power. Two million workers were employed in the construction of airfields and aircraft factories and in stockpiling vital aviation materials. The Lipetsk installation was closed and military flight training was brought home to seemingly innocuous flying schools in Germany.

When Hitler took power the Junkers company had the capacity to produce 18 of its stalwart Ju 52 trimotor transports per year. Milch told it to start building a thousand Ju 52s and a number of trainers. Professor Junkers could see that Germany was going on a war footing and that he was losing control of his own company, and he balked at the order. The impatient Milch, determined to gain outright control of the firm, thereupon resurrected old allegations of fraud at the plant that Junkers had built in the Soviet Union and threatened to banish him from Dessau and his factories forever. Junkers was in his middle seventies and his health

World War I flying ace Ernst Udet (wearing goggles) greets Luftwaffe officers after a 1934 air show at which he demonstrated the Curtiss Hawk (background). The Hawk, an American dive bomber, later became the inspiration for the famous German dive bomber, the Ju 87 Stuka.

With its "inverted gull" wing configuration and greenhouse-like cockpit canopy, the Ju 87 Stuka appears positively ungainly. Yet its effectiveness as a dive bomber was unparalleled and its earsplitting shriek came to be one of the most dreaded sounds of World War II.

was failing, so he agreed—and when the state had his plant it banished him to Bavaria anyway, where he died in 1935.

By the end of 1933 Milch had ordered more than 4,000 aircraft to be delivered by late 1935. Mass production at the beginning included obsolescent biplanes—they would impress the people, they made adequate trainers and their manufacture would build up the industry—but Germany's plane makers were coming up with new designs. Milch's request for an airplane to help Luft Hansa meet the competition of Swissair's new 162-mile-per-hour Lockheed Orion prodded Ernst Heinkel to build the He 70 Blitz in December 1932. This advanced passenger plane, with its fuselage of lightweight duralumin, tested at 234 miles per hour, faster than Britain's newest fighter. By 1935 Heinkel was producing the He 111, a twin-engined, 10-passenger, all-metal monoplane that used a hot new engine from Daimler-Benz and clocked 224 miles per hour in tests. The airplane was a thinly disguised bomber, and its center section, designed to be the bomb bay, was labeled the "smoking compartment" by Lufthansa (which had switched to the one-word spelling of the company's name at the beginning of 1934).

The air force, not satisfied with Heinkel's production rate, ordered him to build a huge new factory capable of turning out 100 He 111s per

Professor Willy Messerschmitt (right) confers with General Erhard Milch under the nose of an Me 109, the plane designed by Messerschmitt that was to become the mainstay of the Luftwaffe fighter force.

month. Claudius Dornier's sleek Do 17, commonly known as the Flying Pencil, was introduced as an airliner in 1934, but its designers had been so intent on speed that they left hardly any room for passengers; it could carry only six people, so few that Lufthansa could make no use of it. It later went into production as a bomber.

Another German plane maker who came to the fore in this period, Willy Messerschmitt, was known for his difficult personality. One day in 1921, his best friend, flying a glider Messerschmitt had designed, was killed in a crash. When bystanders tried to console the designer, Messerschmitt angrily turned on them, shouting, "You can't say it was my fault. I have nothing to do with it. It was his fault." But Messerschmitt had a genius for creating the kind of airplanes Germany needed. In the summer of 1934, when Milch called for a new fighter with the most powerful engine and smallest airframe possible, Messerschmitt produced a sleek, all-metal, four-place monoplane called the Me 109. It edged out the only other serious contender, Heinkel's He 112, and was ordered into production. Messerschmitt continued to improve it, and it was a modification of this plane that later made its mark as one of the all-time great combat aircraft, which would be known to the world as the Me 109E.

One of the most visible, if not one of the most consistent, contributors to the growing air force was a bear of a man named Ernst Udet, a World War I ace who had scored 62 kills as a member of Richthofen's squadron and had made himself famous after the War racing and barnstorming in Europe and South America. Udet had a taste for women, drink, Berlin's fine restaurants and violent stunt flying. He visited the United States in 1933 and flew a Curtiss Hawk dive bomber developed for the United States Navy. Entranced with the plane's handling and potential, he bought two with government funds and shipped them to Germany. Tests convinced the Luftwaffe that it needed a similar plane, and a design competition was ordered for a German *Sturzkampfflugzeug* (literally, "plunge-battle aircraft")—Stuka for short. Heinkel produced one contender, and in the spring of 1936 the Junkers plant turned out the Ju 87, a gull-winged, fixed-gear monoplane that with later modifications would withstand forces six times that of gravity. Udet tested the He 118, crashed it, and after he got out of the hospital, chose the Ju 87. He ordered sirens mounted on the landing gear—"trumpets of Jericho," he called them—to strike terror into those subjected to the Stuka's attack.

In 1935, Hitler boldly and unilaterally canceled the military clauses of the Versailles Treaty—announcing in March the existence of the German Air Force and the introduction of military conscription. From then on the German war machine developed ever more swiftly. The concept of blitzkrieg, the "lightning war" that combined mobile armor with tactical air support, was instituted. Depending on mobility, blitzkrieg made light, fast bombers especially attractive. The enthusiasm of German military leaders for the new doctrine created a peculiar blind spot in their planning: Except for the air force chief of staff, Colonel Walther Wever, almost no one appreciated the need for a heavy bomber.

Wever had been acting as chief of staff since Hitler came to power and was clearly one of the most intelligent officers in the air force, which he had joined after a brilliant career on the Army's General Staff. He soon learned to fly and made a practice of touring Germany's air bases. He usually arrived carrying a big cake in a box and sat down with the flying officers over cake and coffee to discuss problems. Although he agreed with the tactical blitz approach, Wever also understood the airplane's capacity to range over natural defensive barriers and strike vital rear areas. Strategic use of the weapon meant, he said, "the destruction of the enemy's air force, his army, his navy, and the source of supply of the enemy's forces, the armament industry."

When Wever joined the Air Force, Milch gave him Douhet's book, *Command of the Air,* and like Douhet, Trenchard and Mitchell, Wever

"And look, as morning dawns afar, our man has built the Luftwaffe!" reads the caption on a caricature of Air Marshal Hermann Göring drawn by General Ernst Udet, Göring's friend and one of the few men in Germany who could safely make a jest at the Air Marshal's expense.

Und siehe eh der Morgen graut
hat er die Luftwaff aufgebaut!

understood that air power depended on a strong bomber force. He ordered the development of a heavy bomber, and soon a four-engined Junkers Ju 89 and a four-engined Dornier design reached the mock-up stage. Strangely, the program seems to have started without Göring's knowledge. When he first saw the huge Junkers mock-up in the spring of 1935, Göring bellowed, "What on earth is that?" His outburst was taken as a typical fit of temper and work continued on the bombers.

The big planes could have given Germany a strategic bombing force superior to any then existing. But when Wever died in an airplane crash in 1936, the country lost its strongest proponent of long-range bombers. Ten months later, in April of 1937, Göring was to cancel the entire program and thus rob the Luftwaffe of what might have been a decisive weapon. His shortsighted reasoning was based on his fear of Hitler. German factories could turn out five twin-engined bombers for every two four-engined craft, and, said Göring, "The Führer does not ask me *what kind* of bombers I have. He simply wants to know *how many!*"

Despite its many fine aircraft and its remarkable growth, the German air force of 1936 had little depth. It struggled with critical raw-material shortages and severe training problems as it expanded. It was organized for sudden strikes and quick success, not for staying the course of a long war. "The Führer wanted to use the Luftwaffe as a political weapon,"

Menacing Heinkel 51A fighters are seen over Cologne (above, left) and crossing the Rhine (above) during Germany's reoccupation of the Rhineland in 1936. These two groups wear different markings, but they may include the same planes because Hitler used only a few aircraft and had them repainted during the operation to give an illusion of greater numbers.

said Captain Steiner, "long before it was ready as a tactical one."

Totalitarian rule—the capacity of a single man to force action in the absence of the limits that would be imposed by an open, democratic society—facilitated much of the early growth of German air power. But the flaws of one-man rule were evident too: the currying of favor and jockeying for position, the unwillingness to give the leader bad news, the lack of organized procedures that could find flaws and build by plan instead of by whim.

On February 26, 1936, Hitler issued a decree formally creating the independent German air force and dubbing it the Reichsluftwaffe. The full name was never accepted, and it was shortened to Luftwaffe, or "air weapon." Göring summoned a friendly British newspaperman and gave him the full story of Germany's long, secret effort leading to re-armament in the air. He brought in foreign air attachés and told them of the Luftwaffe's advances while some 400 aircraft roared over the Air Ministry building, darkening the sky. Hitler announced to the British Foreign Minister that the Luftwaffe already had achieved parity with the Royal Air Force. This was not true, but the British believed it.

Now the Luftwaffe became a study in exaggeration, a propaganda tool with which to thrill the German people and intimidate potential enemies. False rumors of its strength were started, false information was leaked to journalists, German planes with special engines were passed off as production models when they triumphed at air meets. Foreign visitors were given impressive tours. A French air attaché, suddenly swept into Göring's social circle, reported in detail what he was told about the Luftwaffe's immense advances. Thus when the commander of the French Air General Staff visited Germany, he came prepared to be alarmed, and he was. After seeing the stunning aircraft displays staged for his benefit, the French commander said that if war broke out there would not be "a single French aircraft left after 14 days."

On March 7, 1936, Hitler suddenly translated his aggressive talk into action: The Germans marched into the Rhineland, which had been demilitarized by the Versailles Treaty. Göring worried that "the British and French will come in and squash us like flies," but Hitler answered confidently, "Not if we buzz loudly enough." The Luftwaffe provided the buzz with two understrength squadrons of fighter planes that flew from airfield to airfield on the day of the occupation, changing insignia at each stop to give a magnified impression of their numbers. Signs identifying fictional fighter and bomber wings were posted outside harmless training schools. In fact neither the Luftwaffe nor the Wehrmacht was capable of defending against an Allied reaction, but the thoroughly intimidated Allies did not react.

The easy success of this first overt example of Hitler's expansionist plans, and of the Luftwaffe on which he depended, was to have fateful consequences for the world. "It was the German air force," said American General Carl Spaatz, "which dominated world diplomacy and won for Hitler the bloodless political victories of the late 1930s." ～

Corrosion of an iron man

In the closing years of World War I, airman Hermann Göring was every inch the tough, lean Teutonic war hawk. But during the next 25 years, even as he became the prime architect of German air power, Göring underwent a grotesque personal transformation. As Reich Marshal of the Air, the onetime gaunt fighter pilot was still called the Iron Man, but with a certain scorn. He had become a 280-pound parody of a Nazi brass hat—festooned, a joke of the time said, with "tinsel in front and lard behind." This Göring was aglow with drugs, face powder, nail polish, more than a touch of madness and the unshakable notion that he was, as he once put it, "an inheritor of all the chivalry of German knighthood."

Göring's irrepressible vanity moved him to assemble an immense collection of photographs of himself. The pictures—some of them family snapshots, some taken by his staff photographers, others acquired from the press—filled 47 huge albums by the time they were seized by Allied soldiers from his country home at the War's end.

The photographs on these pages are taken from those albums. They graphically reveal the changes that occurred in Göring. But they also stand as a record of his achievement, documenting his rise to power and his work in bringing the Luftwaffe into being. That achievement was considerable. "Göring has been the creator of the German air force," said Adolf Hitler. "History knows only very few instances of anyone, in the course of a single life, creating a military instrument from scratch and developing it into the most powerful force of its kind in existence."

A combative pilot who never turned down a challenge from an enemy, 23-year-old Göring (right) peers from the cockpit of the twin-engined A.E.G. he flew in 1916.

Amid new Junkers 52s in 1936, Göring's Luftwaffe marks the anniversary of the death of World War I ace Manfred von Richthofen.

Göring (left) and Bruno Loerzer show off the Albatros they flew on a mission that won them Iron Crosses.

Fledgling airman Göring pores over maps.

The Flying Trapezist

One day in 1914, infantry Lieutenant Hermann Göring sallied forth—aboard a bike—on an unauthorized mission to seize the French commander. The mission failed but Göring was commended anyway, for capturing four French infantrymen on his way back.

Such panache demanded wings: Göring was transferred to an air unit. There his agility aloft—amid enemy fire, he leaned out of the cockpit to get low-altitude pictures of the French fortress of Verdun—won him the Iron Cross and a nickname: the Flying Trapezist. He won the Blue Max, Germany's highest military decoration, in 1918 and ended the War with 22 enemy planes to his credit.

Göring (left) and squadron mates doll up a mascot at Stenay Field in 1915.

Appearing the young aristocrat, Göring
visits the casino at Metz in 1916 on his way
back to war after a year spent recovering
from a wound. He had been shot in the
thigh in a dogfight with British Sopwiths.

In action again after being wounded,
Göring (center) briefs other officers of his
new squadron, Jasta 26, in front of one
of their Fokker Dr.I triplanes.

A tense Göring rests after a mission.

Holding the Red Baron's walking stick, Göring takes over Richthofen's squadron in 1918.

Power and opulence

In 1922 Göring came under the thrall of an orator named Adolf Hitler. Göring said Hitler's message echoed his own patriotic zeal "word for word, as if from my own soul." He vowed to the Nazi leader: "I pledge my destiny to you."

He became, in the words of fellow Nazi Josef Goebbels, an "upright soldier with the heart of a child." When Hitler came to power, Göring was given several important positions, including that of Reich Commissioner of Aviation.

His life style came to rival a rajah's. By 1941 he had four opulent homes, a hunting lodge, an income of a million marks a year from his salary and investments, and an art collection growing by the boxcar load. He liked to show it all off while wearing a velvet suit with knee breeches and gold-buckled shoes.

He was once incensed upon opening his own secret police dossier to read, "Göring exhibits many of the signs of a suppressed homosexual and is given to flamboyance in dress and the use of cosmetics." Said Göring, "After all, I'm a Renaissance type."

Göring and wife Emmy look at snapshots with Hitler in 1935.

Göring hugs his pet lion, Mucki, whom he bathed weekly in his own tub.

Wearing a hairnet for a tennis match, Göring confers with his close confidant, Luftwaffe General Ernst Udet.

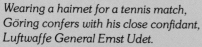

Göring (right) sunbathes by the Baltic with the bearded Italian air minister, Italo Balbo.

Nazi banners and portraits of President Paul von Hindenburg and Hitler surround Göring as he opens the Berlin-Stettin Autobahn in 1934.

As Hitler's top diplomat, Göring pilots his own Junkers 52 transport on a mission to Italy in April of 1933.

Newly named Field Marshal of the Luftwaffe, Göring receives his baton of rank from his commander in chief in 1938.

A crowd cheers Göring and other bigwigs at a Berlin airfield in 1934.

Flying high again

At a 1933 meeting in Berlin, ecstatic pilots who had just heard Göring confide that the air force was secretly being rebuilt carried him around the hall on their shoulders. "Look," one jubilant crony exclaimed, "Hermann's flying again."

Göring inherited a clandestine skeleton air force from the wily generals who had kept it hidden from the Allies. By main force of charm and his clout as Hitler's ramrod, he lured fliers back into harness, coaxed money out of the strapped government, kept plane manufacturers in business and stirred public interest in the air. At last, Göring could exult, "Everything that flies belongs to me!" and bask in the admiration of his comrades. Marveled one, "Something stupendous has been achieved!"

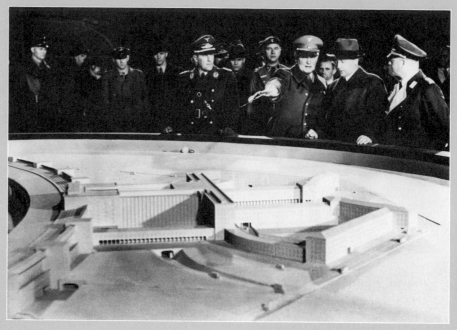

Flanked by his Luftwaffe staff, Göring inspects a scale model of the new Tempelhof Aerodrome south of Berlin in 1937.

During a 1938 state celebration of his 45th birthday, Göring accepts a felicitation from his top adjutant, Erhard Milch.

Hitler, Göring and aide Ernst Udet confer during a Luftwaffe air show in 1938.

Göring gives one of Germany's neighbors, Prince Paul of Yugoslavia, a sobering look at Luftwaffe planes in 1939.

Göring introduces his visitor, Prince Paul, to a deadly German 88-mm. flak cannon, capable of firing 15 to 20 rounds a minute, with a killing range of four miles.

Göring inspects a drill press turning out parts for Stukas—dive bombers—at a Junkers plant in 1939. He frequently paid visits to Germany's aircraft factories to encourage production.

Impressing the world

"I believe in international understanding," Hermann Göring told a cheering crowd of Nazis in 1935. "That is why we are rearming. Weak, we're at the mercy of the world. What's the use of being in the concert of nations if Germany is only allowed to play the kazoo?

"Some people in international life can be made to listen only if they hear guns go off," he continued. "We are getting those guns. We have no butter, but I ask you: Would you rather have butter or guns?" Butter, he said, slapping his belly, "only makes us fat!"

The outwardly cocky Göring privately warned Hitler, however, that it was too soon to use Germany's new air power to achieve the nation's ambitions. Hitler disagreed, banking heavily on the intimidating effect of the Luftwaffe—already overrated by the British and French. The Führer was proved correct when his forces reoccupied the Rhineland in early 1936, and a few months later Göring's creation began its first trial by combat in the Spanish Civil War.

His Luftwaffe now unveiled to a world astounded that the Versailles Treaty had been broken, Göring publicly gives his fliers troop standards at Gatow in 1936.

Under a cloud of Göring's thundering Dornier Do

17s—transports that had been converted into bombers—Nazis in 1937 jubilantly mount their annual Reichsparteitag, a Wagnerian military extravaganza.

4
The Rising Sun takes wing

As the train sped east across the United States in the fall of 1934, newsmen at every major stop tried to get an interview with one of its passengers, a slight, high-ranking but youthful-looking Japanese naval officer on his way from Tokyo to London. But he stayed in his locked compartment, and his aides turned away all inquiries, protesting that the officer did not speak English.

The reporters were interested in the Japanese because of the headlines then being made by Billy Mitchell, who in the twilight of his life was trying to warn America about the growing might of Japan. He was publishing articles with titles such as, "Are We Ready for War with Japan?" and "Will Japan Try to Conquer the U.S.?" Mitchell, who had predicted 10 years earlier that Japan would attack the United States fleet at Pearl Harbor on some Sunday morning in the future, was increasingly strident in his warnings of conflict, and the newsmen wanted the reaction of the reclusive passenger on the train. They also wanted to ask him about his present mission.

For he was Isoroku Yamamoto, the vice admiral of the Japanese Navy who had been selected by Emperor Hirohito to represent Japan at the forthcoming London Naval Conference. At that meeting, existing limitations on the strengths of the world's navies—agreed on at the Washington Naval Conference of 1921 and modified at a London conference in 1930—were to be renegotiated. And it was apparent that Japan, the world's third strongest naval power, was not satisfied with the 5-5-3 ratio of the old agreement, under which Japan could build only three capital ships for every five built by the United States or Britain.

Yamamoto had proclaimed before leaving Japan that during his trip he would read no newspapers lest some devious argument weaken his opposition to what he called "this national degradation." Whether he read the newspapers or not, he was made aware of Billy Mitchell's warnings and finally made a brief statement—in Japanese, as he persisted in his claim to speak no English—in New York, before boarding a ship for London. "I have never thought of America as a potential enemy," he said, "and the naval plans of Japan have never included the possibility of an American-Japanese war." Those who contrasted his

Japan's ambition to be a first-rate air power—for years largely ignored by the West—is reflected in the determined expressions of these cadets at Kumagaya Army Flying School in the 1930s.

calm declaration with the shrillness of Mitchell's writings were much reassured about Japan's intentions.

But on arrival in England, Yamamoto called a news conference and announced (in perfect English that he had polished while getting a Harvard education), "Japan can no longer submit to the ratio system. There is no possibility of compromise on that point." Then, with iron aplomb, he wrecked the naval conference and unshackled the furious growth of the Japanese Navy. In the next seven years Yamamoto would guide that growth in the direction of air power and would personally plan and command the carrier-borne air strike that, on December 7, 1941, would fulfill Billy Mitchell's grimmest prophecy.

Japan was not the only nation strengthening its air power during the 1930s. Air forces throughout the world were girding for war—with varying degrees of success and urgency. The application of air power requires a merging of ideas with hardware capable of carrying them out; the fact that the ideas often were far ahead of the necessary hardware is one reason critics found them so hard to accept. But in the 1930s, technology burst all constraints and the hardware caught up with the ideas. In fact, it did more than that, moving so fast that the most advanced aircraft, the pride of a national air force, were sometimes made obsolete almost overnight, compounding the problems of the planners.

The supercharger, which provides an engine with compressed air to compensate for the lower density of air at high altitudes, vastly increased engine power. The 20-mm. cannon offered savage new firepower, while the development of small, reliable radios made air-to-air and air-to-ground communications routine. Sophisticated new instruments such as radio direction finders and gyrocompasses brought to navigation the precision needed for long-range bombing and night attack.

Designers were progressing rapidly from biplanes to monoplanes, from fabric-covered wooden spars to sleek metal load-bearing skins riveted in place. They were using improved steel and aluminum alloys and were streamlining their designs with enclosed cockpits, retractable landing gear and low-drag cowlings. The first practical variable pitch propellers went into service in 1932 and cabin pressurization in 1937. Between 1919 and 1938, the speed of new warplanes tripled, and runways were improved to keep up with faster takeoff and landing velocities; the days of biplanes bumping off rutted fields were over.

The growth of air power was nowhere more rapid than in Japan, a country that had missed the long experience of the Industrial Revolution that made mechanics part of the heritage of Europeans and Americans. From centuries of medieval solitude, Japan made a breathtakingly rapid leap to modernity: In 1904 it amazed Europe by soundly defeating Russia in a brisk war and emerging as a world-class naval power. The climactic battle of the War, in which the Russian fleet was utterly destroyed in the Straits of Tsushima on May 27, 1904, has been called by one naval historian "one of the most decisive naval actions in history"

Vice Admiral Isoroku Yamamoto, Japan's most forceful proponent of naval air power during the 1930s, later masterminded the attack on Pearl Harbor that brought America into World War II.

General Ikutaro Inoue, a much-decorated veteran of the Russo-Japanese War, took over the Japanese Army air forces in 1919 and promoted their development until his retirement in 1933.

and was the first victory of an Asian navy over a Western one. The young ensign Isoroku Yamamoto lost two fingers in that battle but came away with a deepened sense of pride in his service and his country.

The Japanese military began to study airplanes in 1909. The next year two young Army captains were sent to Europe to learn to fly. Both brought home aircraft and flew them before an enthralled crowd at Yoyogi Field in Tokyo on December 19, 1910. Captain Yoshitoshi Tokugawa covered two miles in four minutes, reaching an altitude of 230 feet. Fully satisfied, the Army opened its first air base, Tokorozawa, some 20 miles from Tokyo and began training five young officers.

Competition between the Army and Navy was especially virulent in Japan, and the Navy immediately sent six officers abroad to learn to fly. The Navy set up a seaplane base at Yokosuka naval port on Tokyo Bay. By 1914 the two services had a total of 28 planes and 25 pilots.

When World War I began, Japan promptly declared war on Germany, in accordance with an Anglo-Japanese agreement, and took over Germany's colonial possessions in the Pacific. At Chiaochu Bay on the Chinese coast, at a time when the idea of bombing ships had hardly occurred to the Western Allies, Japanese planes tried to sink a German cruiser and did sink a torpedo boat. There was little further combat in the Pacific, but Japanese officers studied the conduct of air warfare on the Western Front in Europe and Japanese factories began to manufacture more and more airplanes.

From the start, the Japanese aviation industry, in direct contrast to that of other countries, benefited from heavy capital investments made by major industrialists with full military support and the certainty of huge and continuing orders. Two of the firms that would dominate Japanese aviation, Mitsubishi and Kawasaki, operated shipyards during World War I. In the beginning the civilian factories and those set up by the Army and Navy built European designs—mostly Maurice Farman biplanes—under license. Soon native designs began to appear. Lieutenant Chikuhei Nakajima, one of the first six naval officers trained to fly, retired from the Navy, opened a factory and began producing the Nakajima 5, a two-place biplane, for the Army. Before long, Nakajima, Mitsubishi, and Kawasaki would be the Big Three of Japanese aviation.

Their aircraft were well maintained and skillfully flown, but Japanese commanders had little knowledge of the procedures to follow in preparing their units for combat. To school themselves, they invited two European air missions to Japan after the War, the Army and Navy going their separate ways as usual. A 57-member French group, arriving in 1919, instructed Army pilots in tactical missions—aerial combat, gunnery, reconnaissance techniques and bombing. The pilots learned quickly and the Army readily adopted modern training methods.

Impressed by the Army's progress, the Navy in 1921 brought in a smaller group of former British Navy fliers under Captain Sir William Francis Sempill. This mission spent 18 months at Kasumigaura—the name means Lagoon in the Mist—a huge new naval air base 40 miles

from Tokyo. Sempill's men found the Japanese pilots lacking in mechanical proficiency—they lacked, for instance, the apt mechanic's almost instinctive ability to diagnose odd noises from the engine—but they were dedicated and intelligent and improved their skills quickly.

Japanese aircraft were being built at rates that seemed absolutely prolific compared with the penny-pinching approaches of other nations. In 1920, for example, the Army ordered 300 British Salmsons from its own works and another 300 from Kawasaki. In 1922 Mitsubishi and Kawasaki were asked for 97 French Nieuports and 145 Hanriots. The Navy asked Nakajima and a company called Aichi for 310 copies of a German reconnaissance plane and 250 copies of a British trainer. These were numbers that other nations considered only when they were preparing for an imminent war.

While the Japanese Army's aviation program was forging strongly ahead in the early 1920s, the Navy's languished. The Washington Naval Conference limitations on the building of Japanese capital ships meant that appropriations were sharply reduced, and few Navy commanders saw a significant role for aircraft anyway. But in 1923 Isoroku Yamamoto, promoted to the rank of captain and assigned as executive

His Imperial Highness, the Prince Regent of Japan (in white uniform), inspects the aviation school at Kasumigaura Naval Air Base in 1922. The Prince, who later became Emperor Hirohito, was accompanied by Sir William Sempill (right), chief of the British mission that helped the Japanese develop naval air power.

officer to the naval air base at Kasumigaura, stepped forward to a position of leadership in naval aviation that he would hold until his death. While studying at Harvard during the War he had become intrigued with the military uses of the airplane, intently studying reports of its use in combat, touring American aircraft factories and following with fascination news of attempts to develop an aircraft carrier. He immediately foresaw the significance the carrier could have for an island nation that intended to extend its power across a far-flung ocean empire.

The Japanese Navy was already experimenting with seaborne aviation. In 1914 it had converted the transport *Wakamiya Maru* to a seaplane tender that carried four aircraft and a crane to set them over the side. In 1922 the Navy brought its first aircraft carrier, the *Hosho,* on line. Although the *Hosho* was the world's first carrier to be designed as such (England's H.M.S. *Furious,* the world's first carrier, was converted from a battle cruiser in 1918 and the U.S.S. *Langley,* the first United States carrier, was converted from a collier in 1922), it was for a time a ship without a mission, since no one knew just what to do with it. It was becoming increasingly clear, however, that aircraft could be effective against warships. Japanese observers had been present when Billy Mitchell's planes sank the *Ostfriesland* and in 1924 Japanese planes sank a former Russian battleship in Sagami Bay in a similar bombing demonstration. The Washington Naval Conference agreement permitted the conversion to aircraft carriers of ships that might otherwise have to be scrapped under the treaty, and the Japanese quite legally converted two half-finished hulls—those of a battleship and a battle cruiser—to immense 800-foot-long carriers, the *Akagi* and the *Kaga.* Along with a fourth carrier, the *Ryujo,* they were in operation by 1928, the year the Americans commissioned the carriers *Lexington* and *Saratoga.*

During the 1920s a military clique gained more and more influence in Japan and promoted a growing spirit of chauvinism and imperialism. The country was gradually being closed to foreigners. It took the Americans months, for example, to negotiate limited landing rights for their round-the-world flight in 1924. There were many predictions that the United States was Japan's ultimate target. The influential British editor of a journal called *Aeroplane,* C. G. Grey, forecast war between the two Pacific powers, and Billy Mitchell's visit of 1924—a polite roundelay of Mitchell trying to get information, his Japanese hosts trying to conceal it—led to his report predicting an attack on Pearl Harbor. But such speculation raised no real alarm in the West, partly because of a prevailing arrogant and racially stereotyped view of the Japanese people as myopic, night-blind, accident-prone and lacking in soldiering ability, an attitude the Japanese quietly encouraged as they prepared for war.

By the early 1930s the military was in almost complete control of Japan's government. It intended to dominate Asia and it had already divided up its enemies. The Army would subdue China and fend off the Soviet Union if necessary while the Navy would neutralize the American Pacific fleet. Since China had a modest air force at best and the Army

doubted that the Soviet Union could move many air units to the Far East, Army airmen concentrated on tactical support for ground forces and turned away from the use of heavy long-range bombers.

Yamamoto, meanwhile, was steadily advancing in rank and influence in the Navy. After spending two years in Washington as naval attaché at the Japanese embassy, he had been sent as a delegate to the London Naval Conference of 1930. After his return he was made a rear admiral and head of the Navy's technical branch. His voice was increasingly powerful and his message clear: The Navy's deadliest enemies were the United States's *Lexington*-class aircraft carriers. By 1928 the Americans had three of them, each of which could put 70 aircraft within bombing range of Japan. He wanted land-based aircraft with the range to attack those carriers as far from Japan as possible, and he put Mitsubishi to work on a twin-engined bomber to do the job. The result, the G3M, or Chukoh, later code named Nell by the Allies, took to the air in 1934.

Yamamoto understood that any Japanese naval offensive would depend for success on Japan's own aircraft carriers. He saw that the vessels should be designed to fit the needs of the airplanes they would carry instead of vice versa—a view that shook his ship-oriented colleagues—and under his direction a modern carrier force began to take shape. Now the country's best planes were being designed in Japan. Domestic factories were producing engines that rivaled the world's finest for power and reliability. The Army continued to prize maneuverability over speed and striking power in its fighters and ground-attack

Ground crews ready a squadron of Mitsubishi G3M medium attack bombers of varying designs at Japan's Tateyama Naval Air Station in 1936. At left is a model equipped with a water-cooled engine, and next to it one with an air-cooled engine. The four planes at right have observers' seats located in their noses.

planes. For the Navy, Yamamoto demanded a fast fighter that could fly from a carrier, and Mitsubishi designed one that proved the industry's world rank beyond question: the Type 96, predecessor to one of the world's most famous fighters—the Zero.

Japan was hungry for territory and spoiling for a fight. In 1931 the Army seized most of Manchuria and the following year the Navy attacked Shanghai. The air weapon quickly proved itself in the first fighting. Japanese squadrons bombed and strafed Chinese troops almost without opposition, and carrier aircraft from the *Kaga* and *Hosho* led the attack against Shanghai. One of the first victims was an American pilot, Robert Short, who was in China to deliver a Boeing P-12 and took it up against three Japanese fighters. He lasted two minutes.

Although the conflict was ended by an armistice in just 34 days, Japan maintained a foothold on the Chinese mainland and fighting flared again in 1937. Japan's new status as a world air power was quickly apparent. On August 14, 1937, thirty-eight Chukoh bombers rode a typhoon tail wind across the China Sea from Japan, blasted Chinese air bases 1,250 miles away and returned. Professional airmen around the world realized in surprise that Japanese air power had entered a new era. The Chukoh's 2,700 mile range was more than double that of any other bomber then flying. To achieve it, Mitsubishi had sacrificed armament, armor and even self-sealing fuel tanks (pilots would be told later that a desire for cockpit armor was a sign of cowardice), and the Chukohs proved highly vulnerable to fighter attack.

Still, Japan's air successes were impressive. On a famous occasion over Koitoh a dozen Japanese fighters met 30 Chinese pilots in Soviet Polikarpov I.15 fighters and knocked down 24 with no losses of their own. A pilot named Tetsuzo Iwamoto shot down five Chinese planes during his first engagement, near Nanchang, and became Japan's first ace-in-a-day. Success made the Japanese fliers even bolder. When the pilots of four dive bombers saw that some aircraft had survived their attack on a Chinese airfield, they landed, disabled the remaining planes with machine guns and pistols, and took off before the startled Chinese could return their fire.

These engagements were giving Japanese pilots the kind of confidence and melding of man and machine that comes only with combat experience, and Japan would enter World War II with the most experienced air force in the world. But their technological skill and modern aircraft did not preclude Japanese fliers from maintaining their ancient warrior tradition. Witness a young man named Daisuke Kanbara, who on August 7, 1939, shot down an enemy plane on the border between Manchuria and Mongolia and saw the pilot struggle out after crash-landing. Kanbara landed alongside his opponent and dispatched him—with a traditional Samurai sword that he carried in his cockpit.

At the same time that aviation in Japan had begun striding forward to a steady military drumbeat, the industry in the Soviet Union lay in ruins,

After the Japanese bombing of a Shanghai railway station in 1937, a man in a blood-spattered shirt tries to aid two injured Chinese children. This picture portrayed the victims so poignantly that the Japanese tried to discredit it—almost certainly without grounds—as a fake.

having been destroyed by war and revolution. In early 1918 two determined Soviet scientists changed the course of their country's aviation history when they took their cause to their new dictator, Vladimir Ilyich Ulyanov—better known as Lenin. Lenin had consolidated his control over the October Revolution that had swept the Czar from power the year before but now faced the prospect of a long and bitter civil war between his Red forces and the Whites—Russians who remained faithful to czarist principles and who were allied with the many independent-minded republics of the old Empire that saw a chance to set their own course at last. World War I still raged to the west, although Russia was no longer a combatant.

Against such a background it is perhaps remarkable that the two scientists even got to see Lenin. Their cause was aviation, and they were the two men best equipped to advance it in difficult times. Professor Nikolai E. Zhukovsky, a dignified 70 that year, was a professor at the Moscow Higher Technical School who had founded an aviation society in 1909. He had done original work in mathematics, theoretical and construction mechanics, astronomy and ballistics as well as in his field of aerodynamics. Above all others, he understood the need to put Soviet aviation on a sound scientific basis, and he knew how to do it. With Zhukovsky when he went to see Lenin that day was one of the few other men in the country who had both formal training in aeronautics and practical experience in building aircraft: Andrei Nikolaievitch Tupolev. Just 30 years of age, Tupolev had trained under Zhukovsky at the Moscow Higher Technical School before World War I and had been involved in several aircraft-design projects during the War.

The two scientists explained to Lenin that the Soviet Union's aviation industry had been mortally wounded by the Revolution. The country's skilled aircraft technicians had been scattered, Tupolev told him, and the leading designers (including Igor Sikorsky, who had built his first helicopter in 1909) had left the country as the victorious revolutionaries violently weeded out former and suspected opponents.

If the vastness of the Soviet Union was to be brought and held together, argued Zhukovsky and Tupolev, it must have air transportation and thus a viable aviation industry. They urged Lenin to rescue and rebuild the industry, and their pleas did not fall on deaf ears. The Bolsheviks under Lenin had a vision of wedding their collectivist ideology to science, technology and industry to create a modern power completely different from the feudal aristocracy that had been swept away. Nothing exemplified that view of the heroic future more neatly than air power—and nothing else could be produced so quickly or so visibly. Lenin gave Zhukovsky and Tupolev the authority to act.

On December 1, 1918, they founded the Central Aerodynamics and Hydrodynamics Research Institute in Moscow—called by its Russian acronym TsAGI—which would become the heart of Soviet air research. Professor Zhukovsky gathered about him the best brains still left in the Soviet Union and firmly established both TsAGI and his own reputation as the Father of Soviet Aviation. Tupolev divided his time between duties as chief designer at the Research Institute and overseeing the construction of aircraft elsewhere.

The Russian air force had not distinguished itself during World War I. After serving on the Russian front, German ace Manfred von Richthofen had said that "compared with flying in the West, flying in the East is absolutely a holiday." What the new Red regime was able to muster for its war against the White Russians was weaker still—about a third of the Czar's pilots, their planes disintegrating for lack of maintenance. The Bolsheviks had shot many of the air force officers and put political commissars in charge of those who survived. Military morale and discipline had collapsed. Aircraft plants had been shut down and looted by the workers. But out of this shambles the Bolsheviks began rebuilding

The U.S.S.R.'s airborne aircraft carrier

In the early 1930s, Soviet fighters did not have the range to stay with the bombers they were supposed to protect. Engineer Vladimir S. Vakhimistrov's solution was to adapt the bombers to carry their fighter escort with them.

In December 1931 he tested his first Zveno, or "linked flight"—a modified bomber carrying two fighters atop its wings. Encouraging results spurred four years of development until, in 1935, his grandest version of all lurched into the air—a four-engined Tupolev T.B.3 bomber carrying five parasite fighters.

The monster worked, but, as fighter designs improved, interest in Vakhimistrov's project waned. By the late 1930s the range of Soviet fighters was great enough that the lumbering Zveno became an idea whose time had passed.

A blurred photograph of its only flight shows bomber Zveno-7 carrying four fighters latched to its wings and a fifth dangling below.

In the uniform of a colonel-general, engineer Andrei Nikolaievitch Tupolev displays the decorations of the foremost aircraft designer of the U.S.S.R. Beginning with the ANT.1 in 1921, he designed more than 80 successful military and commercial aircraft.

the air force and managed to stage a limited air display—accompanied by speeches denouncing the West—on May Day of 1918.

Red airmen often were hopelessly outgunned by the White Russians and the units sent by the American and British governments to help defeat the Communists. About a dozen Red planes faced some 100 enemy aircraft on the Archangel front, for example. Yet their air power served the Red forces well, as they fought on several fronts at once in a country severely lacking in railroads. Few as they were, the airplanes provided vital communications and reconnaissance.

During the civil war the Red Air Force learned a lesson that would dominate its thinking for decades. In the Ukraine, when Red infantry troops were about to be encircled by White Russian horse cavalry, flights of 20 to 30 planes bombed the cavalry—with devastating effect because the men could not leave their mounts to take cover. On many similar occasions planes caught horsemen in the open, bombing and strafing them repeatedly. Such successes gave rise to a firm Soviet commitment to *Sturmovik* (ground attack) squadrons—tactical units that 20 years later would deal terrible punishment to advancing Germans. But the other effect of that commitment was a considerable delay in Russia's understanding of the strategic application of air power. Aviation remained a tactical tool of the Army.

The new regime pushed aviation progress with almost religious devotion. TsAGI began offering courses lasting up to three years in aerodynamics, flying, ballooning and aviation mechanics. By 1921 twelve flying schools had opened and Soviet leaders boasted that they had 350 planes on the line and plenty of pilots to fly them. Osoaviakhim, a paramilitary organization of air enthusiasts, quickly gained some three million members (within a decade its membership would jump to 13 million). It organized civil-defense training, provided gliding and flying club facilities, coordinated the training of technical specialists and administered a national savings drive that funded the purchase of more than 100 aircraft for the Air Force. Osoaviakhim eventually would establish more than 21 flight-training centers for sport aviation (the Air Force supplied instructors), 40 complete airports, more than 100 simple landing fields and extensive repair shops. It even built its own aerodynamics laboratory. When the Red Air Force became interested in paratroopers—it would create the world's first paratroop assault division in 1934—Osoaviakhim made parachuting a major Soviet sport.

During the 1920s aircraft and engine factories gradually reopened, despite the shortages of raw materials, lack of skilled workers, a scarcity of machine tools and excessive meddling by bureaucrats. Engine plants remained integrated as they had been before the War: Every part from piston to crankshaft was produced in a single factory. By Western standards the industry was primitive, but it was growing.

The cooperation between the Soviet Union and Germany that made possible the early growth of the secret German air force was also of critical importance to the Soviets. The two German air facilities that

On a 1937 tour of RAF bases, German General Erhard Milch examines the gunner's position of a British Wellesley bomber.

While British bomber crews stand at attention, Milch and his Luftwaffe colleagues inspect rows of aircraft at Mildenhall, an RAF base 60 miles northeast of London.

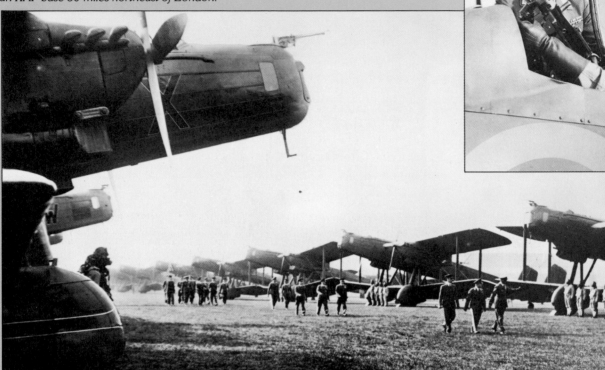

General Italo Balbo (in civilian dress) arrives in England with other Italian officers for a military air show in 1928.

Showing the hardware to potential enemies

During the two decades between world wars, the leaders of every major air force kept a wary eye on the state of military aviation in other nations. And as the 1930s progressed, their interest became ever more intense. A major war seemed to be almost inevitable, and few of them doubted that much of the coming conflict would be fought in the air.

There was surprisingly little secrecy among these potential enemies vying for air supremacy. Well-publicized aviation expositions, showcases for the most advanced engines and planes, were open to all comers. Rival air forces often exchanged visits and proudly displayed their latest bombers and fighters.

In a way, such demonstrations were a game of bluff in which nations sought to impress one another with their air power. But to some German airmen, the game seemed to be getting out of hand: In 1936 a rival of Luftwaffe General Erhard Milch denounced him for treason, claiming that Milch had disclosed too much detail about German air strength to a delegation from Britain's Royal Air Force.

General Massenet de la Maraucourd of France (left) arrives at an RAF base in 1935 with a flight of French bombers.

were opened in the Soviet Union were accepted with the understanding that the Soviets would have full access to them. Tupolev observed design techniques in the Junkers warplane factory at Fili and while there designed his first aircraft, the single-seated ANT.1 monoplane. The Germans trained Soviet officers at the secret air base at Lipetsk and some Soviets went to Germany for special instruction. After a few years most of this cooperation ended, but not before it had well served the interests of both countries: The Germans were able to develop the nucleus of their Luftwaffe away from the prying eyes of the Allies, and the Soviet government then took over the Fili and Lipetsk installations, with their wealth of excellent equipment and facilities.

Soon the Soviets were producing increasing numbers of both aircraft and engines of native design, including those of Tupolev and, in 1922, the first of many fighters designed by Nikolai Polikarpov. But the Soviets continued to copy the foreign aircraft and engines that they liked—sometimes under license, sometimes not. Indeed, Polikarpov's last major fighters in the late 1930s, the I.15 biplane and his first all-metal monoplane, the I.16, looked so much like American fighters that they were widely known in the Spanish Civil War by American names: The I.15 was taken for a Curtiss fighter and the I.16 for a Boeing fighter. Meanwhile TsAGI continued to turn out experimental designs.

The growth of Soviet air power in the 1930s was marked by a new determination as enemies arose on all sides: To the east, Japan entered China and Mongolia, and to the west Hitler's Germany was becoming more threatening. In 1928 Soviet factories had turned out about 1,000 aircraft and the Red Air Force had 15,000 people. Four years later the industry, employing some 120,000 workers, had doubled production, and the Air Force had increased the number of personnel to 50,000. The national air academy turned out some 150 aviation scientists and commanders each year, and flight training improved steadily. Large-scale combat exercises with massive ground armies became routine. More training academies were opened, research was stepped up and the number of frontline aircraft steadily increased. By the outbreak of World War II, the Soviet Union's capacity to build aircraft was equal to that of any other air power in the world except the United States.

But its advances were overshadowed by the setbacks it suffered during the violent and wide-ranging purges begun by Stalin late in 1934. Half the ranking officers of the Air Force were killed or imprisoned, including the commander in chief. The universities were depleted; leading designers were eliminated; TsAGI was crippled. The brilliant Tupolev spent five years in Siberia with an execution order hanging over his head. K. A. Kalinin, who had done advanced work on the swept-wing concept, was shot when a plane of his design crashed, killing four party members. (Punishment for failure in the air industry was not new. Years earlier, Polikarpov and Dimitri Pavlovich Grigorovich had designed the I.5 fighter while in prison on charges of sabotage. The excellence of the new design earned them their freedom.)

The purges destroyed whatever chance the Red airmen had of building a truly first-rate force. Morale was shaken and caution became the byword, with political reliability the primary criterion for promotion to command. The general staffs of both the German and the Japanese Armies characterized Soviet air leadership as crippled.

Among the most important effects of the purges was the Air Force's loss of a promising long-range bombing capability. A strategic bomber force was organized in 1936 at the insistence of the chief theoretician of the Soviet Air Force, General Vasili Vladimirovich Khripin. Khripin had written an introduction to a Russian translation of the works of Giulio Douhet and had become an advocate of an independent bomber force charged with strategic missions far behind enemy lines. Tupolev's T.B.3 four-engined bomber, with its two-ton payload and its 839-mile range, was the vehicle Khripin's doctrine required. The T.B.3 had first flown in 1930, and more than 800 were eventually built. But after Khripin disappeared at the height of the purges, Soviet interest in long-range bombers waned and the emphasis returned to tactical ground support.

Thus it was a cautious, disorganized and inexperienced air force that held the responsibility for extending Soviet power into the skies in 1936. But it was a huge force nonetheless, and events in Spain would soon give it an eagerly awaited chance to test its strength and its doctrines.

Twenty years of peace were drawing to a close. More and more authorities were coming to believe that the aggressive expansion of Germany and Japan would lead to armed conflict, and everywhere the tempo of preparations for war—and especially war in the air—increased.

In Britain the RAF had retained its independence: Hugh Trenchard had made sure of that through his long tour as chief of staff, which had continued until 1929. His fundamental idea that offense was the key to air power, and that only an independent bombing force could maintain the offense, was deeply ingrained in the RAF, and two thirds of its frontline aircraft were bombers. But development of new British bombers lagged until news of the secret Luftwaffe slipped out in 1934. Then it did not take long for the aircraft industry to produce results—the four-engined Stirlings and Halifaxes, the twin-engined Manchester, which in time was given four engines and was called the Lancaster, and Vickers' Wellesley, which evolved into the 265-mile-per-hour Wellington.

It was partly the speed of such bombers that led to the need for a new fighter that could keep up with and protect the bombers and could intercept similar bombers being produced by other countries. The Air Ministry issued specifications in July of 1934, asking for the design of a fighter fast enough to catch—and armed heavily enough to destroy—any bomber. The plane was to be a monoplane with retractable landing gear, enclosed cockpit, a ceiling of 33,000 feet and speed of at least 275 miles per hour. It was to be armed with eight American high-speed Browning .303 machine guns mounted in the wings, firing outside the propeller arc. Supermarine, a company known throughout the world for its extremely fast seaplanes, agreed to take on the project.

Britain's premier designer of high-speed aircraft, Supermarine's Reginald Joseph Mitchell, spent the winter of 1934-1935 in the Austrian village of Kitzbühel in the hope of improving his health. He had known for a little more than a year that he had cancer and that his prospects were not good. Mitchell had become the chief engineer at Supermarine in 1920, at the age of 25. During the next 11 years he had designed the fastest floatplanes in the world; they won the prestigious Schneider Cup three times. Mitchell and his design team had tried to adapt the best features of their seaplanes to the design of a day-night fighter requested by the British Air Ministry in the fall of 1931, but in three tries they were not successful. While in Austria he came to know a group of young German glider pilots and from their exuberant conversations he became convinced that the emerging Luftwaffe was a far greater threat to Britain than anyone in his country realized. He hurried home, imbued with the need to help meet the threat in the time he had left.

The resulting aircraft was the Spitfire, destined to become one of the most famous fighters in the world. When it first flew on March 5, 1936, a spectator described it as a highly polished silvery monoplane that looked almost ridiculously small behind its huge wooden propeller. It was powered by a new Rolls-Royce engine, the Merlin, which was to become famous in its own right. The aircraft's advanced streamlining, retractable landing gear and distinctively elliptical wings made it an unforgettable sight, and its performance, which matched or exceeded all Air Ministry specifications, left the test pilot chortling with delight as he climbed out of the cockpit after that first flight. The RAF promptly ordered 310 Spitfires—within a few years it would order more than 4,000—but in June of 1937, before the first plane was delivered, Mitchell, his cancer incurable, died. He was remembered by a colleague as a man "who was always trying to peer just over the horizon."

With its new designs for fighters and bombers and its independent air force organized for strategic missions, Britain had at least the foundation on which to build a response to the threat of air war. Such was not the case elsewhere in Europe.

France had possessed the world's largest air force at the end of World War I, but the nation had suffered over six million casualties and could summon no enthusiasm for modernizing its capabilities to fight another war. Its leaders adopted a defense policy based on the heavily fortified Maginot Line just as air power made such fixed defenses entirely obsolete. A separate air ministry was created in 1928, and in 1933 the air force took the title Armée de l'Air, adopted distinctive uniforms and proposed dividing itself into tactical and strategic forces, but in actuality an interservice committee remained in control and the Army's Chief of Staff vigorously opposed any strategic role. The issue went unresolved for years, and the air force, despite its title and uniform, remained decentralized and firmly limited to ground support.

Preoccupied with their vulnerable location, the French had always

An Italian bomber with its wings removed for shipment is off-loaded on the Red Sea coast.

Ca.101s and SM.81s—wings striped to aid the spotting of downed airmen in the desert—crowd an airfield in the Italian colony of Eritrea.

Testing ground for Il Duce's bombers

As new, faster planes were developed during the 1930s, air forces bandied about bold but unsubstantiated claims as to their effectiveness in warfare. In 1935 Italian dictator Benito Mussolini, eager to build a colonial empire, seized an opportunity to give his aircraft a real trial: He invaded Ethiopia with 10 divisions supported by a force of nearly 400 planes.

Ethiopia's 12 aircraft offered little resistance. A more serious obstacle was the 500,000-man Ethiopian Army—poorly equipped but expert at fighting in the rugged mountains around Addis Ababa, Ethiopia's capital city. Italian surveillance planes kept tabs on them, and Caproni 101 and Savoia-Marchetti SM.81 bombers pummeled them with gas and shrapnel bombs whenever they clustered.

To the delight of Il Duce, the air strikes were an unqualified success—with the embarrassing exception of 40 bombs dropped on a Red Cross unit by his own son Vittorio. But 270,000 other bombs were dumped on the Ethiopians, and the Italians advanced steadily, capturing Addis Ababa seven months after launching the invasion.

A salvo of lightweight bombs hits an Ethiopian camp.

Ethiopian mountain people run from the path of a landing Italian Ca.101 bomber.

felt that strategic bombing invited retaliation, a belief that had prompted their resistance to the British Independent Bombing Force during World War I and lessened postwar interest in bombers. The industrial turmoil of the 1930s—the government nationalized the aircraft industry in 1936—further hampered progress. As a result, the large French air force was deteriorating as those of other countries were improving.

Although Italy had given the world its premier prophet of strategic air power, Giulio Douhet, the Italian policies of the 1930s reaffirmed the truism that a prophet is not without honor save in his own country. The Italian government did reinstate General Douhet after the War and did establish a separate air force—the Regia Aeronautica—in 1923, but its military planners did little to implement Douhet's ideas. The head of the Regia Aeronautica, the redoubtable Italo Balbo who startled the world in 1933 when he led a formation flight of flying boats across the Atlantic, was an early advocate of strategic bombing. But the air force he built turned out to be a tactical organization, in accordance with dictator Benito Mussolini's concept of a modified blitzkrieg. The Breda 65, a two-place fighter also used as a light bomber and reconnaissance aircraft, typified the inadequate equipment with which Italy's air force faced the growing threat of war: In sardonic tribute to its handling characteristics, pilots called it the *ferro da stiro*—flatiron.

In the United States, Billy Mitchell's ideas prevailed, and the industrial and technological might of the country was producing the hardware needed to give them substance. He had believed that the air weapon had an offensive and strategic mission—that it should be primarily a long-range strike force. He destroyed himself in advancing his ideas, but they took hold even in the face of increasing isolationism and the economic depression that impoverished the Army. Hardly was Mitchell out of the way when the Army Air Corps was created, giving the air weapon at least an organizational status on a par with those of the infantry or cavalry, even if the Army's top brass was reluctant to accord it the same importance. The Navy sped up the expansion of its own aviation program lest the Army try to take over its role. The result was an outstanding fleet air arm—carriers and excellent carrier aircraft—that caused Japan to regard the United States as its most formidable opponent.

Army airmen, in analyzing their future role, focused on the long-range bomber. America's remoteness from potential enemies reduced the threat of invading armies that dominated European military thinking and consequently reduced the pressure to concentrate air power in a tactical ground-support role. But the great distances involved also made the development of an offensive bomber force more challenging.

In 1932, America's first modern bomber came on line—the Martin B-10, an all-metal monoplane with twin engines, enclosed cockpits and machine-gun turrets fore and aft; it could fly at 212 miles per hour with a 2,260-pound bomb load. In 1933 the War Department called for the design of a heavy bomber with a range of 2,000 miles and speed of 250 miles per hour. Martin proposed a modification of its successful twin-

In an impressive display of precision long-distance navigation in 1938, two B-17 Flying Fortresses intercept and make a simulated bombing run on the Italian liner Rex some 700 miles from New York. The flight was intended to demonstrate the Air Corps's ability to defend America's coasts.

engined B-10. Douglas offered the DB-1, a spin-off from its DC-3 airliner, which was then on the drawing boards. Only Boeing proposed a four-engined aircraft, its model 299, also an adaptation of a transport. This aircraft would become the best bomber in the world and one of the great aircraft of all time—the B-17 Flying Fortress.

The organization to bring the strategic mission together with the long-range bomber was set up in 1935. Called the General Headquarters Air Force, it was an independent strike force, part of the Air Corps but operating directly under the highest command levels. It was almost exactly what Billy Mitchell had been demanding 15 years earlier.

In 1936 the world's air forces, for all their technological wizardry and bold intentions, consisted mostly of young men flying new aircraft according to untested tactical and strategic theories. But in the events of that year three of the air forces found a rare chance, which the others observed with rapt intensity, to conduct a laboratory test of their untried war-making apparatus under battlefield conditions. Partly because of their participation, what might have been a minor rebellion in a country racked by frequent changes in government became instead the Spanish Civil War, a crucible in which were tempered many of the air weapons that the great powers of the world were forging. ～

A generation of warplanes in search of a war

Combat aircraft, like the pilots who fly them, need a war in order to win lasting glory. Most of the fighters and bombers developed during the 20 years between World Wars I and II had relatively little opportunity to prove their worth in battle and thus have been largely forgotten by all but avid aviation buffs. Yet many of these warplanes—14 of them are presented here with the dates of their first flights, and with aircraft on facing pages in scale to one another— were hot performers and important steppingstones in the evolution of air power.

The single-seat open-cockpit biplane continued to dominate military aviation for more than a decade after World War I—a time when few countries had either money or enthusiasm for new weaponry. But progress, at first barely trickling its way through official indifference, soon reached flood stage. Wood spars and fabric covering, still found in the Hawker Fury, gave way to the all-metal construction of the Boeing P-26. Even the best of biplanes, among them the Fiat C.R.32, were slowed by their extra wing and a profusion of bracing, and could not keep up with monoplanes such as the Tupolev S.B.2.

The Polikarpov I.16 and the Martin B-10 gained extra speed by retracting their landing gear after takeoff, thus reducing drag. Some of the planes, like the Mitsubishi aircraft shown here, were driven by muscular air-cooled radial engines, while others were fitted with the new generation of sleek, powerful, in-line, liquid-cooled engines, such as the Rolls-Royce Kestrel engine in the Hawker Fury. Aircraft silhouettes began to bristle with armament and antennas, evidence of increasing firepower and the new ability to coordinate and guide missions by radio.

Their time in the spotlight was brief; they figured in few decisive conflicts—the Spanish Civil War being the most notable exception. But these planes enabled designers to refine many features that made the aircraft that eclipsed them faster, tougher and even more deadly.

HAWKER FURY FIGHTER (GREAT BRITAIN, 1928)
With its wood-and-steel framing sheathed partly in fabric, partly in metal, the Fury embodied construction methods of past and future. This one was flown by the RAF's No. 43 Squadron, the "Fighting Cocks."

BOEING P-26 FIGHTER (UNITED STATES, 1933)
Low-wing monoplane design and all-metal construction made the P-26 a trailblazer despite its drag-inducing wing bracing and fixed landing gear. This one wears the colors of the Army Thunderbirds Squadron.

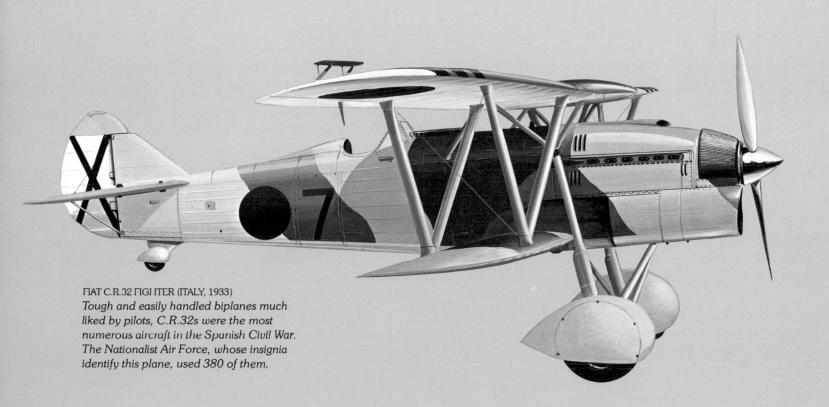

FIAT C.R.32 FIGHTER (ITALY, 1933)
Tough and easily handled biplanes much liked by pilots, C.R.32s were the most numerous aircraft in the Spanish Civil War. The Nationalist Air Force, whose insignia identify this plane, used 380 of them.

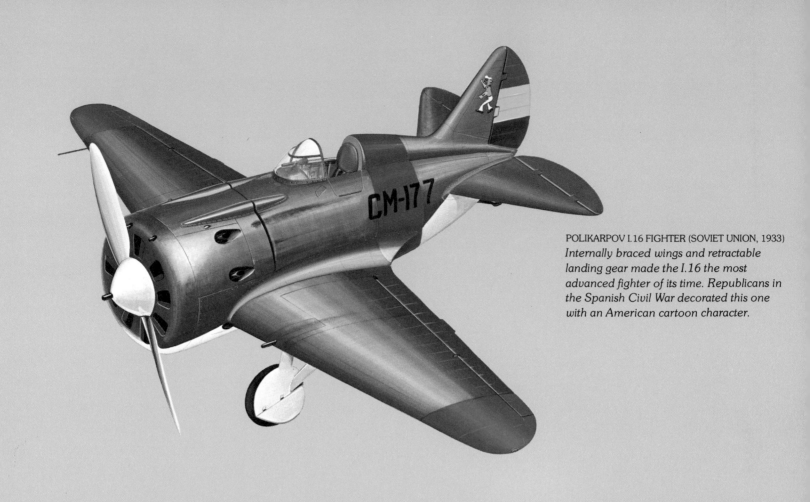

POLIKARPOV I.16 FIGHTER (SOVIET UNION, 1933)
Internally braced wings and retractable landing gear made the I.16 the most advanced fighter of its time. Republicans in the Spanish Civil War decorated this one with an American cartoon character.

DEWOITINE D-510 FIGHTER (FRANCE, 1932)
The D-510, shown here bearing the insignia of France's Armée de l'Air, was a beautifully streamlined, high-altitude, all-metal fighter with a cantilevered low wing. It was the first French machine to top 250 mph.

HEINKEL HE 51 FIGHTER (GERMANY, 1933)
A cleanly designed and sturdy biplane, the He 51 was the leading manifestation of the resurgence of German air power. This one was flown by the Richthofen Wing, named for the famous World War I ace.

MITSUBISHI A5M FIGHTER (JAPAN, 1935)
Forerunner of the legendary Zero, the A5M was an effective carrier fighter. The Japanese characters proclaim that this aircraft was bought for the 12th Air Group by a patriot from Osaka named Arimoto.

BREGUET XIX BOMBER (FRANCE, 1921)
Shown here in the markings of the Armée de l'Air, the Breguet XIX was a versatile and reliable fabric-covered metal biplane. It became one of the most widely used military aircraft of its generation.

SAVOIA-MARCHETTI SM.81 BOMBER (ITALY, 1935)
The SM.81 trimotor bomber, which also served as a transport, was used extensively in Italy's African colonies. The bright Italian air force markings helped rescuers spot a plane downed in the desert.

MARTIN B-10 BOMBER (UNITED STATES, 1932)
With two engines, retractable landing gear and internal bomb bay, the B-10 represented America's increasing interest in long-range bombers. It won the 1933 Collier Trophy for aeronautical advances.

JUNKERS JU 86 BOMBER (GERMANY, 1934)
*The Ju 86 was both the Luftwaffe's
first effective bomber and a widely used
transport. The blue band denotes this
aircraft's role with the Blue Force, the name
given one side in a war-game exercise.*

VICKERS WELLESLEY BOMBER (GREAT BRITAIN, 1935)
*One of Britain's first monoplane bombers, the
Wellesley had an extremely long, 74-foot
wingspan that gave it great range. One of its
two under-wing bomb-carrying panniers
can be seen in this RAF Squadron 76 aircraft.*

MITSUBISHI G3M BOMBER (JAPAN, 1937)
The G3M's resemblance to the Ju 86
reflects Mitsubishi's close association with
Junkers. But the G3M was an all-
Japanese product designed to defend the
homeland against enemy aircraft carriers.

TUPOLEV S.B.2 BOMBER (SOVIET UNION, 1934)
One of a Russian breed of medium bombers
that normally flew for the Republicans
in the Spanish Civil War, the S.B.2 shown
here was captured by Franco's forces
and repainted with Nationalist insignia.

"We bombed it and bombed it and bombed it"

On July 25, 1936, three men arrived in Berlin after a grueling two-day flight from Spanish Morocco aboard a Junkers transport. One of the travelers was Captain Francisco Arranz of the newly formed Spanish Nationalist air force; his companions were Adolf Langenheim and Johannes Bernhardt, German businessmen who had formed an outpost of the Nazi Party in the Spanish Moroccan city of Tetuán. They carried with them a desperate appeal for German help from General Francisco Franco, the emerging leader of a military uprising against Spain's Republican government.

The revolt had started a week before, and almost half of Spain was already in the hands of the insurgent Nationalists. But the other half, including the capital city of Madrid and some of the richest industrial regions, remained under the government's control. The uprising seemed to stand midway between success and failure.

A Nationalist victory—which would wrest Spain from the left-leaning Republicans and align it with Europe's Fascist nations—depended on Spain's Army of Africa, a crack force made up of the Spanish Foreign Legion and Moroccan troops. Franco had won the allegiance of these tough soldiers away from the government, but they were isolated in Morocco, across the Strait of Gibraltar from Cádiz. In between lay the Spanish Navy, its ships seized by loyal Republican sailors who had killed or imprisoned their Nationalist-sympathizing officers and were prepared to sink any vessels carrying the Army of Africa to Spain.

Franco clearly needed outside support, but cautious German diplomats were dubious about aiding the Spaniard. Not only did they fear reprisals against the many Germans living in Spain but they knew that other European powers would not look kindly on German intervention in Spain's internal affairs. Nazi Party officials liked the idea, however, and Admiral Wilhelm Canaris, Chief of Military Intelligence, who had visited Franco several times in Spain, recommended him as a "tested man" who "deserves full trust and support." That was enough to get Arranz and his two German colleagues an audience with German Chancellor Adolf Hitler the same evening in the Bavarian city of Bayreuth, where the Nazi hierarchy was attending the annual music festival

The German pilot of a Ju 87B Stuka dive bomber plunges toward a target in Spain in early 1939. The Stuka was one of many aircraft that were combat-tested during the Spanish Civil War.

honoring composer Richard Wagner. Hitler had just heard a performance of Wagner's *Siegfried* and his mood was buoyant; he listened with mounting enthusiasm as Franco's emissaries pleaded their case.

Hitler quickly determined that he would quietly aid the Spanish Nationalist cause, and would start by sending a fleet of transport planes to carry Franco's stranded troops to Spain. Later, Hitler explained that his actions were designed to help thwart the "danger of the Red Peril overwhelming Europe" and to ensure Germany a steady supply of favorably priced Spanish iron ore. For Field Marshal Hermann Göring, the Spanish excursion offered something else as well: It was, he said years afterward, an opportunity "to test my young Luftwaffe."

At 5 a.m. on July 27 an unarmed Junkers Ju 52 took off from Berlin's Tempelhof field. A veteran Lufthansa pilot, Captain Alfred Henke, was at the controls. Henke paused at Stuttgart, where he took on extra fuel tanks, and then flew nonstop the 1,250 miles to Tetuán in Spanish Morocco, arriving early the next day. With hardly a pause, Henke took 22 fully armed Moroccan soldiers on board and ferried them to Seville, which was held by the Nationalists. On his second trip, the Junkers groaning, he took more than 30 Moroccans. The world's first large-scale airlift of troops in wartime was under way.

Shortly after Henke left Tempelhof, 19 more Junkers transports left Germany for Morocco and Spain. They had been commandeered from Lufthansa, complete with their flight crews. By then the Luftwaffe had formed Special Staff W—named for the staff's commander, Lieutenant General Helmut Wilberg—to handle Spanish affairs and to deflect any questions that might arise about the secret operation. An earnest though still minimal German military effort had begun. In addition to the airlift, it involved a corps of 86 volunteers who would go to Spain by ship with six crated Heinkel He 51 fighters and twenty 20-mm. antiaircraft cannon to protect the transports.

To explain the movement of so many men, the Luftwaffe set up a "tourist organization" called the Union Travel Society. The young volunteers assembled on July 31 at Döberitz, where one of their officers told them that their mission was to save an entire people from Bolshevism. General Erhard Milch himself was there to see them off. They traveled to the North Sea port of Hamburg, where they boarded the steamship *Usaramo,* whose hold was bulging with the Heinkels, antiaircraft guns, munitions and other equipment. At 1:30 a.m. on August 1 the ship quietly slipped its moorings; by dawn it was well out to sea.

The Luftwaffe men spent their time relaxing and playing cards; then, on August 6, with all lights dark, the *Usaramo* ran the Spanish Republican blockade into Cádiz. Within minutes the Heinkels were being unloaded for the trip by train to Seville. At a Spanish airfield there, German riggers began assembling the fighters while their pilots fretted and gunners set up their artillery pieces to protect the field.

Day by day more troops and supplies arrived on the big Junkers trimotor transports—their Lufthansa markings scoured off their corrugated skins. Back and forth they winged, some planes making up to seven flights a day. The Germans called the venture Operation *Magic Fire,* a title that must have seemed appropriate to the airlifted Moroccan troops, most of whom were getting their first airplane ride. When the airlift ended two months later, the planes had delivered 13,523 soldiers and 593,914 pounds of matériel, including 36 artillery pieces and 127 heavy machine guns. Now Franco had in place a highly professional army with which he could attempt to seize control of Spain.

Spain's Left and Right Wings had been locked in a contest of strength for years. The Left had narrowly won the 1936 elections and formed a government made up of Republicans, Socialists and a small minority of Communists. The Communists were the most disciplined of the factions on the Left; they were under the direct control of Moscow, and there could be little doubt that they would seek to subvert the government and bring it into the Soviet orbit. On the Right was a coalition of monarchists, the regular Army, most of the Catholic hierarchy and a group of political parties, among them the Spanish Falange. Named for the Mac-

Spanish Moroccan infantrymen in Franco's Army of Africa wait on an airfield in Tetuán, Morocco, to be flown to Seville in 1936. The hard-working Ju 52 trimotor transports supplied by Hitler carried as many as 35 men each, though designed to hold only 17.

edonian military formation that had destroyed Greek democracy in 300 B.C., the Falangists admired the Italian Fascists and German Nazis, but they were nevertheless a separate and unrelated group.

The Left and Right had come into open conflict on July 13, when a prominent Rightist leader was murdered by government police. When the news reached Las Palmas in the Canary Islands, to which Franco had been semiexiled by the new government, the 44-year-old general—who sympathized with the Falangists—got ready to move. On July 19 he flew to Spanish Morocco, where he would soon take command of a full-scale military revolt that would be known to history as the Spanish Civil War.

From the very start, the War had a quality of mindless ferocity that would have a stunning emotional impact on world opinion. Troops on both sides pillaged and raped. Corpses piled up, churches were burned, families were broken, old grudges were settled and Spanish blood drenched the dry Spanish soil. After the initial violence had left the country divided roughly in half *(map, right)*—and after the German airlift brought in Franco's army—the rebellion became a classic modern conflict with massive armies clashing in the field and aircraft contesting command of the skies. A transfixed world watched, fascinated and horrified, as contending forces marched and countermarched through a bitter conflict that would drag on for nearly three years.

Spanish blood and bone alone could not have sustained such fighting for so long. What made the brutal War go on and on were the arms, technical assistance and men that were supplied to both sides by other nations that saw Spain as an arena in which to test weapons and tactics in preparation for a world war that loomed ever more clearly on the horizon. Britain, the United States and to some extent France hovered on the sidelines in hopes of avoiding the larger war. But the Soviet Union, Italy and Germany participated directly. In terms of air power, these belligerent nations would make Spain a proving ground for theories developed over the past two decades and more. Not since 1918 had men fought in Western European skies; now they would begin unleashing for the first time the full fury of 20th Century aerial warfare.

The original German volunteers had orders to fire only if fired upon. It was soon apparent, however, that Franco could not win without more spirited help. Then Franco came up with conclusive evidence that Soviet aid was reaching the Republicans: Russian markings were found on fragments from a bomb dropped on a Nationalist airfield. Germany responded with an outpouring of equipment, weapons, ammunition and aircraft into Spain.

At the center of the German war effort was the elite Condor Legion, which had been organized within months after the first transport planes were dispatched to Morocco. By November the first hand-picked volunteers were on their way to Spain, and the Condor Legion soon solidified into an effective combat air force of some 6,000 men well supplied with aircraft. The Legion included ground support—antiaircraft batteries

A triumphant Generalissimo Franco returns the salute of an honor guard at the military headquarters in Burgos on September 29, 1936, just after Spain's ruling junta proclaimed him head of the Nationalist government and commander in chief of the insurgent forces.

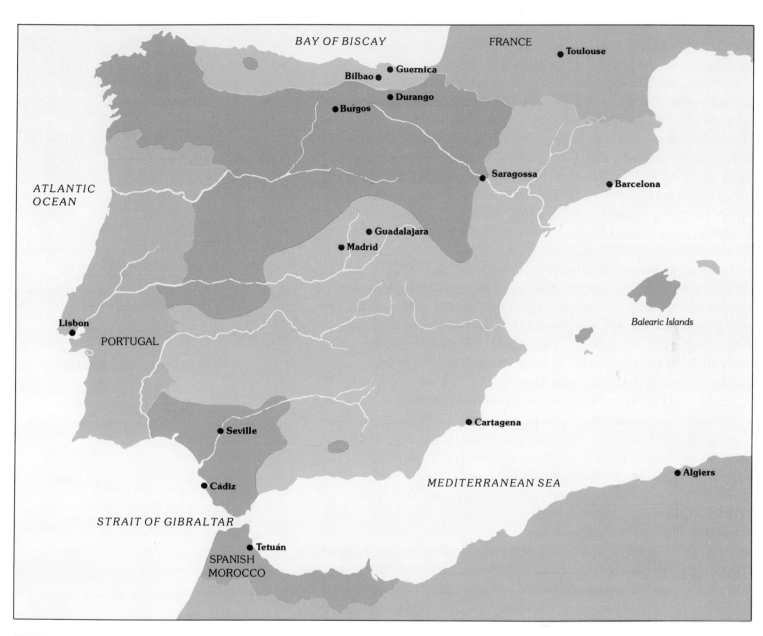

In August 1936, Spain was divided roughly between Nationalists in the northwest and Republicans in the south and east. But the Seville airlift had given Franco a foothold in the south, and Republican Basques threatened the Nationalist rear from the far northern region.

Areas under Nationalist control

Areas under Republican control

with 20-mm. guns and the excellent new 88-mm. artillery, plus service units and two companies of light tanks—but its reason for being was air power. It converted the 20 Ju 52 transports into bombers and had 14 He 51 fighters and a few attack and reconnaissance planes. More and better airplanes continued to arrive by sea.

In keeping with the clandestine nature of Germany's aid to Franco, the men of the Condor Legion wore Spanish-type uniforms. They shuttled in and out of Spain in utmost secrecy. All their letters home were funneled through a central office and bore a deceptive return address: Max Winkler, Berlin, S.W. 68. But Luftwaffe men noticed, as Adolf Galland put it years later, "that one or another of our comrades vanished suddenly into thin air without our having heard anything about his transfer orders, and that after about six months he returned, sunburned and in high spirits. He bought himself a new car and in the greatest secrecy told his more intimate friends the most remarkable stories about Spain." Galland, too, would serve in the Condor Legion and then go on to become one of Germany's leading World War II fighter pilots.

Germany was not alone in its contributions to the Nationalist air arm. Franco's agents had also appealed to Mussolini's Fascist government for assistance, and on July 30 the first detachment of Savoia-Marchetti SM.81 trimotor bombers had set out for Morocco with their Italian markings painted over and the crewmen in civilian clothes. Like the Germans, the Italians wanted to play down their role in the growing conflict, and they were aided in their deception by their Spanish allies: When an Italian plane crash-landed in French Morocco, a Spanish aircraft flew over soon afterward and dropped a package containing Spanish Foreign Legion uniforms. A message in Italian read: "Put these on and tell the French you belong to the Legion stationed at Nador."

Soon Italy was in the Spanish War in considerable strength. It sent in a ground force that numbered up to 60,000 men at one point and established the Aviazione Legionaria to conduct air operations, beginning with three bomber groups of three SM.81 squadrons each, a like number of fighter groups flying swift and agile Fiat C.R.32s, a light bomber group, various reconnaissance and attack aircraft, antiaircraft batteries, supply and maintenance crews and radio operators.

By far the greatest amount of air-power assistance to the Republicans came from the Soviet Union. On September 10, 1936, the first Red Air Force technicians reached southeastern Spain and made ready for the arrival of 18 Polikarpov I.15 biplane fighters that were being loaded onto the freighter *Bolshevik* at Odessa. Another dozen I.15s were transferred at sea to a Spanish Republican vessel. By the end of September, Russian ships had put 200 pilots and 1,500 technicians into Spain, as well as 31 twin-engined Tupolev S.B.2 bombers and tons of supplies and munitions. Then on October 16, Colonel Yakov Smushkevich, who would become famous in Spain under the pseudonym General Douglas, arrived with 150 more Red Air Force personnel, including 50 fighter pilots who put the I.15s into the air as soon as the planes left the riggers' hands. Later that month a squadron of speedy Polikarpov I.16 monoplane fighters reached northern Spain.

The Soviets were somewhat more successful at concealing the help they gave Spain than were the Germans and Italians. Their international organization, the Comintern, orchestrated a worldwide flood of propaganda that planted an impression of Fascist nations overwhelming Republican Spain with the brutal weight of their superior arms. In fact, however, the Soviet-backed Republicans held their own in air power against the German- and Italian-supported Nationalists until the end of 1937, when Soviet interest in the Spanish Civil War began to wane.

France's Left-inclined government of the period was instinctively sympathetic to the Republicans and at the outbreak of hostilities supplied some aircraft, though none comparable to that of the other powers. André Malraux, the famous French novelist, organized an interna-

Field Marshal Hugo Sperrle, whom Hitler described as Germany's "most brutal-looking general," flies to Spain aboard a Junkers 52 to take command of the Condor Legion in 1936. Sperrle was instrumental in building the Luftwaffe and later helped plan the Battle of Britain.

At a Condor Legion airfield in Saragossa, Spain, German technicians load bombs into Heinkel 111 medium bombers. The sleek, twin-engined planes could carry up to 4,410 pounds of bombs and had a top speed of more than 250 mph and a range of about a thousand miles.

tional squadron of French planes for service in Spain, where he was a central figure in Madrid during the early months. Later Britain and the United States pressured France to embrace a noninterventionist policy aimed at keeping the war in Spain from erupting into a wider conflict. But numerous individual Britons, Americans, Frenchmen and men of many other nationalities fought for the Republican side. Most of these volunteers were organized into the famed International Brigades and saw desperate and bloody service in the ground armies. Others served the Republicans as combat-aircraft pilots, and together with their Russian fellow fliers they quickly showed the Nationalists—and the watching world—the devastating effects of modern air power.

On March 8, 1937, Franco's ground forces launched an attack on Guadalajara, at the foot of the Guadarrama Mountains 30 miles northeast of Madrid. Victory would give the insurgents a new route by which to attack the capital. Some 30,000 motorized Italian troops led the advance. The Italians made up a formidable force: The soldiers rode in trucks, some 70 to each battalion, and were supported by 250 tanks, 180 cannon, 50 fighter aircraft and a dozen reconnaissance craft. Swiftly they rolled down a narrow macadamized highway, eating up kilometers as the Republican troops fell back in suspiciously good order.

As the attack began, heavy rain soaked the clay roadsides; then the temperature fell, the rain turned to sleet and ground fog appeared. Rising water took out a bridge and stopped part of the column while the leading vehicles rolled on along the highway. Nationalist air support was based well to the north, beyond a high ridge that now was banked in clouds. A few fighters found their way through the clouds and fog, but most turned back, leaving the attacking troops without adequate air cover. So it was that Soviet planes operating from nearby airfields faced almost no opposition when they came in under low clouds to attack the tanks and trucks strung out on the highway.

There were perhaps a hundred Soviet fighters—the compact Polikarpov I.15 biplane, which the Spanish Republicans called *Chato,* or snubnose, and the roaring I.16 monoplane, which they called the *Mosca,* or fly. There were also a number of bombers. The aircraft swept along the undefended highway in waves. One of the bomber pilots was an American named Eugene Finick, who had been among the first volunteers. Later, from a hospital bed where he was recovering from burns and wounds, Finick described how the action looked from the cockpit of an attacking aircraft.

"We tore that rolling, mechanized offensive into ribbons," he wrote. "You looked down on that dark, endless column and it seemed as if they'd keep going from sheer physical weight. We came over, squadrons of fifteen in close formation. We dumped every bomb we had on the tanks in front and the road—tons of high explosives. We dropped them flying low, so there was no mistake about where they'd hit. In two minutes time the tanks and the road were a shambles. The tanks were blown up, overturned, piled up in knots." As the attackers raked the column with machine-gun fire, Finick saw enemy troops "jump from their tanks, leap by the hundreds from the motor trucks and run." They looked like "little dark shapes, twisting, turning, knocking one another down in their madness to find shelter."

Burning tanks and trucks plugged the road. Vehicles that left the road in an effort to escape mired down in the sodden clay. The side roads, built for farm wagons, collapsed into gumbo under the heavy vehicles. Then the Republican infantry struck the demoralized Italians and drove them back. Retreat turned abruptly into rout as streams of soldiers, abandoning vehicles and weapons, poured back over the ground they had taken, Republican planes harassing them as they went.

The Battle of Guadalajara did more than deny the Nationalists an access to Madrid. It also helped convince commanders on both sides that air power was best employed for tactical support of ground operations; throughout the Spanish Civil War, strategic bombing of enemy strongholds and population centers would be viewed as an incidental role for the air weapon. The battle also accelerated the efforts of both sides to field superior planes and changed the way some aircraft were used in combat. The German He 51, for example, was so thoroughly outclassed as a fighter by the Soviet I.15 and I.16 that it was soon diverted to service as a ground-attack plane, using 22-pound bombs, and was under strict orders to avoid encounters with enemy fighters.

Spanish pilots flying He 51s developed the chain formation, in which they flew in a long line, the leader striking first and then flying around to tag onto the rear of the line. The resulting chain of aircraft could subject ground gunners to incessant heavy fire and thus suppress antiaircraft defenses until, on signal, the planes all broke off at once and headed for home. So consistently did the Spanish Nationalists use this technique that they adopted a linked chain as part of their insignia.

Some pilots considered flying ground attacks a little shameful. Adolf Galland, who flew He 51s himself throughout his tour in Spain, likened ground-attack squadrons to "poachers who do not use their weapons decently, as true hunters do." But there was danger enough from ground fire below and enemy fighters above, and many of the fliers found their work wildly exciting. Oloff de Wet, a British volunteer who flew ground attacks for the Republicans, remembered vividly that as his squadron swooped down, "red berets, lorries, trees, the khaki coats of the running men are coming to meet us. It is like blowing on a plate of sand, the grains are scattering, leaving the road naked and white." The plane seemed to shiver almost in ecstasy, de Wet said, as he pressed the trigger release. And then: "I can see flecks of flame on the leading edge of my wing. Could any life be as good as death like this? Gently I ease on the stick. The world is moving round me—trees, houses, roads, villages, slip underneath the belly of my machine. The horizon falls like the edge of a blue blind suddenly drawn down, and I am climbing heavenwards. The day-bleached face of the moon peeps

Perched on the bumper of a truck equipped with a motorized crank, a German Condor Legion mechanic prepares to start the engine of a captured Russian fighter plane, the formidable Polikarpov I.16. Flight tests of such aircraft helped German pilots assess enemy capabilities.

Supporting ground forces advancing on Barcelona—probably in 1938—two Italian Savoia-Marchetti SM.79 bombers drop their deadly cargoes on the city's defensive positions. Barcelona finally fell to the Nationalists in early 1939.

from beneath my wing. The sweet metallic flavor of blood is on my tongue as my nose bleeds."

Of course, patrolling fighters from both sides were quick to engage planes attacking ground forces, but it was difficult to pinpoint an aerial quarry on large and fluid battlefronts. The ground-attack planes flew low, struck in an instant and roared away. And for the men caught on the ground—on both sides—the attacking planes were fearsome weapons, as an anonymous member of the XV International Brigade remembered later. The onslaught started with a low and distant hum that grew louder until it became "a roar that filled the air, that almost lifted you up, shaking." Then the planes swooped down and let loose their bombs: "The whole earth was blasted into pieces. It heaved and

Puffs of smoke blossom in Durango as German bombers assault the defenseless road and railway junction on March 31, 1937. Nearly 250 civilians were killed.

rocked and swayed and roared and smoked, and the bombs kept coming down, and every time you heard that whistle and scream you knew there was a shaft pointing to the small of your back.'' The bombing run was followed by strafing. ''Everything was smoke and dirt and dark but you knew the machine guns would see through the dark, and everybody around you was killed and you were left here alone and the next burst would catch you square across the back.''

For all its ability to inspire such terror—and to annihilate enemy soldiers—the He 51 was so slow and ponderous that the Germans became soured on biplanes. Their interest soon shifted to the new Messerschmitt 109 monoplane, the first production models of which came into service in Germany in early 1937. The Fiat C.R.32, on the other hand, was such an excellent fighter that the Italians were seduced into continuing confidence in biplane designs. The Fiat was an extraordinarily robust aircraft, very fast and steady in the all-important diving attack. It had an impressively threatening look, too. As Oloff de Wet described it: ''The oval radiator under the propeller looks like the mouth of some small, ugly, gluttonous fish.'' The Fiat was the best fighter in Spain until the Soviet I.16 arrived, and even then it remained effective.

153

The greatest ace on either side, Joaquín García Morato, flew a Fiat for the Nationalists through most of the War and was passionately devoted to it. Normally a warmhearted, easygoing man, García Morato in combat was a deadly and instinctive pilot. He had fought in Spain's Moroccan wars in the mid-1920s and had become a brilliant aerobatic pilot. He was vacationing in England when Franco's uprising began and he chartered a plane and flew home to take up the Nationalist cause. He soon organized a squadron, drew Fiat No. 3-51 and proceeded to run up a record score: In 511 sorties he engaged in 144 dogfights and shot down no fewer than 40 enemy aircraft with 12 more probables. No one on either side came close to García Morato's total, and his luck would hold until a week after the War ended, when No. 3-51 stalled in a stunting climb and spun into the ground, killing him instantly.

The gull-winged I.15, or *Chato,* looked so much like the American-built Curtiss Hawk that Nationalist pilots, who were much more familiar with American aircraft than with Soviet planes, called it the Curtiss. The I.16, or *Mosca,* which had outclassed the Fiat, resembled the Boeing P-26; for a while, the Nationalists referred to it as the Boeing. Stubby and dangerous, it scurried across the sky behind its snarling radial engine and soon the men who had to fight it gave it a new name—*Rata,* or rat. Until advanced Me 109 models arrived late in the War, the I.16 was the fastest fighter in Spain and also had the highest ceiling.

Frank Tinker, the most successful American pilot in the Spanish War—he scored eight kills for the Republican side—was the first non-Russian to take the I.16 into combat. He wrote later of his initial sortie in this deadly fighter: "I looked down and saw a Fiat fighter right behind one of our biplanes. I threw my plane into a right half-roll and was down behind the poor Fiat before he even knew it. My first burst of bullets set fire to his motor and my last got the pilot as he stood up and started to jump. I didn't intend to shoot the pilot but I was still a little unused to my new plane and couldn't seem to get out of gear once I started firing."

In the late spring of 1937, alarmed by the heavy toll of downed He 51s, the Luftwaffe rushed out the latest model of the Messerschmitt 109—the Me 109B. But these early Messerschmitts were lightly armed and not clearly superior to the enemy's aircraft. Indeed, the first time Tinker saw one he shot it down.

He had heard rumors of the new German monoplanes, and a few days later he saw three of them attacking a Republican biplane. "I managed to get on the tail of the leading enemy monoplane," he wrote, "and pumped bullets into it until it burst into flames." His two squadron mates brought down another Messerschmitt while the third Luftwaffe pilot streaked for safety. A year later, however, the Condor Legion had begun to upgrade its fighter fleet by replacing the Me 109B with the Me 109D, immediate forerunner of the magnificent Me 109E of World War II. Now German fliers would all but rule the Spanish skies.

Even so, Russian fighters sometimes maintained local air superiority, and a later German assessment would conclude that neither side ever held total command of the air. But the Russians rarely ventured far beyond their own lines; most of the action was carried to them by marauding Nationalist aircraft. Gigantic dogfights often developed—sometimes there were 50 planes to a side, occasionally as many as a hundred—and tactics were not so different from those of World War I. Altitude was still priceless. Pilots maneuvered to put the sun behind them and then slashed downward in attack—"they came and were gone like the mysterious hand of God," said Oloff de Wet in his description of an attack of He 51s.

But the aerial engagements differed markedly from those of World War I in at least one respect: These planes were much, much faster than any flown in that earlier conflict. At times the action was concluded before a pilot was sure what had happened. Francisco Tarazona, a Spanish Republican flying an I.16 on his first combat mission, saw his wingmate firing and caught a glimpse of planes ahead. His Russian instructor's admonitions rang in his ears: Maneuver constantly to avoid being picked off. "I try not to fly horizontally for a single minute," he recalled later, "I dive, climb, turn sharply and do some half-rolls." Then he looked around and found that his plane was totally alone in the sky. Back at the base, his mechanic asked, "How was the battle?" But Tarazona was not even sure that there had been a battle.

A Spanish pilot on the Nationalist side, José Larios, the Duke of Lerma, an elegant, fun-loving young nobleman, caught the fragmented quality of these aerial duels when he exuberantly described what he called his "Red-letter day." As he and his fellow fliers came over some mountains they saw the enemy *Ratas* and *Chatos* massing ahead. The spirited battle began immediately, as each pilot sought out his victim. "A *Rata* shot down across my nose," Larios recalled. "I swung in behind her and got in a fleeting burst as she dived away. Another one streaked by with a Fiat 200 meters behind. I gave her a burst of crossfire to keep her going. A *Chato* came at me, head on, and we both opened up simultaneously, shot past each other, and banked over hard to reach each other's tails. The circle tightened rapidly. After the second round the Red pilot gave up and dived. This was the opening I was waiting for. Down I went after him in a vertical dive and closed up fast, pouring in bullets. Dense black smoke streamed back, and the stricken machine began to spin; it hit the ground close to the Ebro River."

Later that day, on a second sortie in his Fiat C.R.32, Larios became engaged in yet another round of swirling aerial combat. After blasting one I.15 out of the sky he turned to another that was hot on the tail of a fleeing Fiat. "I struck fast and just in time. I dived on them and began firing from a distance to get the Red pilot off his victim," he recalled. "He broke away and dived to the ground. I followed him down with the full advantage of superior altitude and closed up rapidly, giving him short, sharp bursts at point-blank range. Seconds later smoke poured out."

Such fighting ended the tight, three-aircraft V formation that had been favored by military aviators in peacetime flying; in combat, pilots

A cry of rage from the victims

Unable to defend their cities from the destructive onslaughts of Nationalist bombers in the Spanish Civil War, the Republicans turned to propaganda to bolster the will of their people and to generate sympathy for their cause.

After the first bombing raid on Madrid in November of 1936, a devastating onslaught that went on nonstop for three days, the Spanish government and various allied groups published a flood of posters that angrily portrayed the attack on civilians as an atrocity. While some of the wording was contradictory—the poster at top right advocates building more bomb shelters while the one at bottom right urges evacuation—the propaganda helped channel the horror of the people subjected to this new kind of warfare into stiffened resistance to the Nationalists.

MADRID
THE "MILITARY" PRACTICE OF THE REBELS

4 -21
35

WHAT EUROPE TOLERATES OR PROTECTS
WHAT YOUR CHILDREN CAN EXPECT
MINISTERIO DE PROPAGANDA

A Spanish government poster distributed throughout Europe to protest the bombing of civilians shows a young child with an identification tag around her neck menaced by a phalanx of Nationalist bombers.

criminals

SOCORS ROIG

POUM

A grief-stricken woman clutching a dead child screams "criminals" at bombers overhead in a poster published in Barcelona by Spain's second-largest trade union, a group known by its acronym, POUM.

CAMARADAS de la RETAGUARDIA
MAS REFUGIOS y EVITAREMOS
NUEVAS VICTIMAS

Bombs bearing the insignia of German and Italian fascists plunge toward a fallen youth in a Republican poster that advises, "Comrades of the Rear Guard: More shelters and we will avoid new victims."

A dramatic portrayal of Madrid in flames supports an appeal to evacuate the city. Despite the advice from the Commission of Defense, Evacuation Committee, most citizens stood their ground.

EVACUAD MADRID

using it spent so much time watching one another's positions that they had too little time to look for enemies. As an alternative formation, Condor Legion pilots developed the *Rotte,* or loose pair, in which one plane flew lead with the other covering it from 200 yards behind and to the side. Two *Rotten* made a *Schwarm*—two aircraft flying in attack positions, their outboard wings covered by two tail men. It made a devastating combination, and the Luftwaffe as a whole soon adopted the new formation. Later, the British and American air forces adopted it too, calling it the "finger four" because of its resemblance to the finger-tips of an outstretched hand.

Not all German innovations were so successful. That old slow trimo-tor, the Junkers 52 transport, had been transformed into a bomber but proved to be dangerously inadequate. At 150 miles per hour it was an easy target for antiaircraft gunners and was full of blind spots open to fighter planes. Before he moved on to Fiats, José Larios was a bombardier-gunner in a crankdown turret that had been improvised between the wheels of a Ju 52. Until bomb racks were installed he would sit with his legs dangling from an open hatch and drop the bombs as they were handed to him by other crewmen. After the racks came into use he could bomb from his turret, reaching overhead to pull release levers at the right moment, then seizing his machine gun to fend off enemy fighters.

Buffeted by cold winds, Larios rarely knew he was under attack until he heard the "metallic tattoo of machine guns cutting through the deep roar of the engines." Then a fighter would explode into view and Larios would squeeze off a quick burst before it disappeared. "They looked like bright wasps," he wrote of a swarm of I.16s, "with their brilliant red markings and dark green fuselages." But too many Ju 52s were going down in flames, and the planes were soon reserved for night missions or for days when very heavy fighter cover was available.

As a replacement, the Germans chose the swift, twin-engined Hein-kel He 111, a first-class medium bomber. Together with the Italian Savoia-Marchetti SM.79, the new plane wiped out the Soviet advan-tage given by the 250-mile-per-hour Tupolev S.B.2 bomber, which had appeared in large numbers during the early months of the War. (This aircraft resembled the American Martin B-10, so Nationalist pilots usual-ly called the planes Martins.)

On both sides, however, bombers were used primarily to support armies, not to achieve strategic goals beyond victory in specific battles. Indeed, the first concentrated aircraft bombing of a major city in history, the repeated assaults on Madrid, was carried out in hopes of opening the Spanish capital to a Nationalist army that was at its gates. For three days in late November, 1936, wave after wave of Condor Legion bombers pounded the city with high explosives and incendiaries. The assault was continuous: Night bombers were guided in by the fires and ordered to bomb where the city was still dark. The Telefonica, the city's huge telephone exchange and a major public building, was hit again and again, as were a number of hospitals. More than 150 people were killed and many more were injured; hundreds were left homeless.

Apart from the fact that its purpose was primarily tactical rather than strategic, the raid was the first exercise of air power against a population center as envisioned by Giulio Douhet and Billy Mitchell. German officers, in fact, viewed the raid partly as an experiment to test the effects of bombing on civilians. Strangely, though, the reaction of Madrid's populace was far different from the expectations of the apostles of aerial bombardment. The people were not induced to surrender by the bursting bombs and raging fires; they were not even demoralized. Instead, from different parts of the city, like a rumbling drum, came the defiant cry of Republican resistance, chanted syllabically by thousands of voices: *"No pa-sa-rán! No pa-sa-rán! No pa-sa-rán!"* — "They shall not pass!" And they did not pass: When the bombing stopped, the Nationalists were no closer to taking Madrid than they had been.

The devastation of Madrid was chilling enough. "Oh, old Europe, always so occupied with your little games and your grave intrigues," wrote a Madrid-based French newspaper correspondent in his diary. "God grant that all this blood does not choke you." But the following year brought an even more graphic demonstration of air power, foretelling as it did the brutal nature of the larger war that all but the most devout optimists feared would soon engulf Europe.

The little market town of Guernica was especially significant to the Basques, the proud and distinctive people of the northern mountains of Spain. Here, near a huge oak tree whose dead and weathered trunk had become a virtual shrine to the cause of Basque liberty, Spanish monarchs traditionally had come to pledge their respect for the local rights of the region's residents. Now, in the warm spring of 1937, the northern campaign of the Spanish Civil War was momentarily focusing on the historic town. Nationalist troops were approaching from the south and Republican troops were falling back toward Bilbao to the west; many of them were certain to be swarming across Guernica's small stone bridge over the Oca River.

Guernica—or at least its bridge—was thus deemed a legitimate target, and at 4:30 p.m. on April 26 the town's church bells pealed to announce an air raid. Townsfolk, farmers and refugees from the nearby fighting began moving into makeshift shelters that were little more than cellars with sandbags at their doors. Then a German bomber made an exploratory pass, scouting the town's defenses. Finding that it had none, the pilot dropped a stick of high explosive to signal the attack.

He was followed by wave after wave of He 111s and Ju 52s escorted by a strong fighter force. The bombers swept in to strike and restrike every 20 minutes. Explosions leveled rows of wooden buildings. The front wall of the Julian Hotel fell, exposing four floors. The end of the railway station collapsed. A hospital was hit; doctors, nurses and wounded soldiers died together. Stone buildings heaved and crumpled.

Silver-colored two-pound thermite tubes, then a novelty of war, tumbled down like schools of glistening minnows. They crashed through rooftops and split open, each pouring out 65 grams of flaming molten metal that dripped from floor to floor, igniting all that it touched.

Soon people struggled out of their cellars as flaming buildings began to collapse on top of them. But once out in the streets they became targets for the He 51 fighters that appeared suddenly at rooftop level. Huge and deafening, their hammering machine guns scouring the pavement, the planes caught men, women, children and animals as they ran in panic; bodies were thrown about as if by chopping blades.

Not until dusk, at about 7:45 p.m., did the last plane depart. George Steers, a London *Times* correspondent on the scene, detected "the nervous crackle of arson" throughout the town. And then, he wrote, "the total furnace that was Guernica began to play tricks of crimson color with the night clouds."

Guernica was left a charred shell. Fully a fourth of those who were there that afternoon were casualties: Some 1,600 people were killed and nearly 900 were injured. Nationalist troops entered a few days later without serious incident. Colonel Wolfram von Richthofen—chief of staff of the Condor Legion and cousin of the famed World War I ace, Manfred von Richthofen—reported to Berlin that the attack was a great success. But Adolf Galland said later that the men of the Condor Legion were ashamed of destroying a defenseless town and killing so many innocent civilians. Not even among themselves, he claimed, did they like to talk about Guernica.

The world press, under no such restraint, reacted in a sustained burst of shock and outrage. Startled at this response, the Nationalist government and the Condor Legion declared that Guernica had not been attacked; the Basques, it was said, had torched their own town for propaganda purposes. Then a London *Sunday Times* correspondent asked a Nationalist officer about the raid. The officer's answer would burn in the consciousness of the world: "Of course it was bombed. We bombed it and bombed it and bombed it and *bueno, why not?*"

For all the destruction, however, two landmarks remained unharmed. The remnant of the great symbolic oak of the Basques was not touched. And neither was that little stone bridge.

Franco was less enthusiastic about bombing cities than were his German and Italian allies and some of his own officers. He intended, after all, to win the War and did not relish the prospect of ruling a nation that had been largely destroyed from the air. It has been said that he was furious when he learned of the toll at Guernica; he was equally angered in early 1938 when the Italians bombed Barcelona without informing him. During that attack, planes struck every three hours for nearly two days, killing some 1,300 citizens.

The assault on Barcelona—like the earlier raids on Madrid and Guernica—had little discernible effect on the course of the War, which by mid-1938 was nearing a conclusion. But if the bombing of cities was not

High scorers in the trial by combat

Three countries embraced the opportunity provided by the Spanish Civil War to test their recently developed warplanes in combat. At first the largest contingent of aircraft was that provided to the Republican forces by the Soviet Union, whose Tupolev S.B.2 bombers and Polikarpov I.15 and I.16 fighters performed well but were soon obsolescent. Italy furnished the Nationalist side with Fiat C.R.32 biplane fighters and Savoia-Marchetti SM.79 and SM.81 bombers; all were well-liked aircraft, but only the SM.79 continued in extensive service after the Civil War.

The country whose experiments in Spain yielded the most notable results, then and later, was Germany, the first and most ardent of the outside participants. The Condor Legion, organized and manned by Luftwaffe personnel, took Germany's newest and most promising planes into battle on behalf of Franco's Nationalists.

When the testing under fire was over, three types of aircraft—shown here in Nationalist markings flying combat missions over Spain—emerged as the star performers in the Luftwaffe's arsenal. With slight modifications, such as more armament for the Messerschmitt Me 109 (whose three machine guns proved insufficient in Spanish combat) and more streamlining for the Junkers-built Stuka dive bomber and the Heinkel He 111 bombers, they went on to become major participants in World War II.

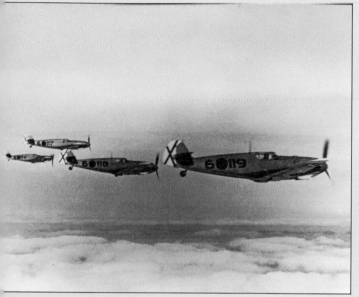

A squadron of the Condor Legion's formidable Messerchmitt 109s patrols over Saragossa in 1939. A subsequent version of the Me 109 became a paramount fighter of the Second World War.

A Stuka dive bomber reaches 400 mph in its dive prior to releasing its bombs. Its performance as a close-support weapon in Spain endeared it to Luftwaffe planners.

An He 111 bomber, faster than most fighters in Spain, hits a Republican position.

proving decisive in Spain's civil war, the specter of ravaged Guernica would soon have a critical influence on events far from the Condor Legion's field of battle. For Hitler, his dreams of conquest quickened by his unopposed occupation of the Rhineland and by his recent annexation of Austria into the German Reich, now coveted the Sudetenland, a region of Czechoslovakia that was largely inhabited by ethnic Germans. When his claims to this disputed territory were turned aside by the Czechs, Hitler threatened to seize it by force. Britain and France, fearful that this squabble might erupt into another world war—and that London and Paris might go the way of Guernica—prevailed upon Hitler to negotiate with them for a peaceful settlement of the Sudeten question. The Czech government was excluded from the talks.

On September 29, 1938, the Prime Ministers of Britain and France joined with Hitler and Mussolini to sign the so-called Munich Agreement, which gave Hitler a virtual free hand in the Sudeten matter. The vaunted might of the German Luftwaffe, with its implied threat of an awesome exercise of air power—if fewer than 50 bombers could destroy Guernica in a few hours, what could thousands of planes do to a major city in a few days, weeks or months?—had yielded Hitler yet another bloodless victory over his European rivals.

Franco's victory in Spain would hardly be bloodless, but it came soon enough. Emboldened by the policy of appeasement adopted by Britain and France at Munich, Hitler stepped up his aid to the Nationalist cause. The dispirited Republican forces gave up city after city, province after province, until at last, on March 28, 1939, a column of Nationalist troops marched unopposed into Madrid. The Spanish Civil War was ended, and the officers and men of the Condor Legion were soon on their way back to Germany, there to ponder the lessons that had been learned in the crucible of Spain.

Unfortunately for Hitler's soaring ambitions, the major lesson that his Luftwaffe drew from the Spanish experience turned out to be erroneous. The success of backing up ground troops with tactical air support—and the indifferent benefits obtained from large-scale urban bombing—led Luftwaffe planners to downgrade the importance of long-range strategic bombing. Richthofen, while he could applaud the havoc wrought at Guernica, became a passionate believer in the doctrine of ground support, and as he rose rapidly in the Luftwaffe he carried his views to ever-higher levels.

The knowledge that the Soviets had drawn the same conclusions would be of little consolation to the Germans during the war years that were soon to come. For Britain and the United States, their military planners unhindered by combat experience in Spain, would later turn to strategic bombing with a vengeance unmatchable by a Germany still wedded to the ways of a previous conflict.

Indeed, as early as September 1938, while the Condor Legion was still soaring through Spanish skies, President Franklin D. Roosevelt

Dressed in their distinctive olive brown uniforms, men of the battle-tested Condor Legion parade past German Chancellor Adolf Hitler in Berlin in June of 1939, after their return from Spain. With Hitler on the reviewing stand is the Legion's new leader, Colonel Wolfram von Richthofen.

called a meeting of his top military men. As an Assistant Secretary of the Navy during the World War I era, Roosevelt had opposed most of Billy Mitchell's ideas, but now he had taken a new tack. As Harry Hopkins, his close adviser, put it later, the President was "sure then that we were going to get into war and he believed that air power would win it." Roosevelt informed his startled subordinates that he wanted an air force of 10,000 planes. Billy Mitchell's old friend General Henry H. "Hap" Arnold, who had just become chief of the Air Corps, pointed out that it took more than just aircraft to make an air force. Men, training, matériel and tactics would also be required. Roosevelt nodded and settled for 6,000 airplanes. But in less than two years, Roosevelt would be calling for the production of 50,000 military airplanes per year as American factories poured out aircraft for beleaguered Britain.

The capacity to project military power through the air at any target in virtually unlimited strength was approaching reality. What had been an almost experimental adjunct of war a mere two decades earlier had become the key to making war. The Italian visionary of air power, Giulio Douhet, may have been wrong about numerous particulars, but he was right on the single point that counted: Air power would alter the nature of warfare—and change the world forever. 〰

War's new horrors: death from the skies

Measured against the appalling carnage that resulted from ground action in the Spanish Civil War, the loss of civilian life from aerial attack was modest: some 5,000 to 10,000 killed—1 to 2 per cent of the War's total dead.

Yet nothing in the War so shocked public opinion as the use of air power against noncombatants. In the air attacks on Madrid, Bilbao, Barcelona, Valencia and, above all, Guernica, a watching world saw with terrible clarity what the wartime fate of civilian populations had become. Adding to the terror was the random nature of the Spanish bombing. Neither side had a consistent policy governing civilian raids—although both were reluctant to destroy the cities of a country they hoped to rule. Accordingly, the heaviest raids were carried out by the Nationalists' German and Italian allies, frequently without General Francisco Franco's approval.

While air attacks on Barcelona and Madrid were predictable, raids like the one on the town of Granollers that left 100 women and children dead seemed terrifyingly haphazard. Towns without military garrisons or defenses were under attack as early as March 31, 1937, when German Junkers bombers slaughtered 248 civilians at Durango, in a grim foretaste of the fury that a month later would destroy Guernica.

For those repeatedly under bombardment, terror gradually gave way to a fatalistic will to resist. "Knowing you could be killed at any moment from the air, you thought you might as well die fighting," recalled a secretary who survived the siege and bombing of Madrid. The attitude surprised German officers of the Condor Legion—and foreshadowed the heroic resistance of civilian populations under the bombs of World War II.

A fast bomber squadron of Italian Savoia-Marchetti SM.79s soars over the spare landscape of central Spain on a 1937 mission against the town of Villanueva de la Cañada. A high-speed plane with medium range, the SM.79 was the chief Italian bomber in Spain from 1937 on.

The helplessness and horror felt by civilians are written on the faces of these villagers fleeing an air attack west of Madrid in 1936.

After a 1937 bombing attack, citizens of Madrid look to the wounded, paying scant attention to the dead sprawled before a row of shuttered shops.

Flames set by incendiary bombs rage through the apse of Guernica's Church of San Juan. The attack on the town constituted the first major use of incendiaries against an urban center.

The burned-out shell of Guernica smolders after being struck by an estimated 100,000 tons of German bombs. Some 70 per cent of the buildings in the towns were completely destroyed in the raid.

Acknowledgments

The index for this book was prepared by Gale Linck Partoyan. For their assistance in the preparation of this volume, the editors wish to thank John Batchelor, artist *(pages 134-141)*, Louis S. Casey, consultant *(pages 134-141)*, Walter Roberts, cartographer *(page 147)* and John Young, artist *(endpaper and cover detail, regular edition)*.

For their help with the preparation of this book, the editors also wish to thank: **In East Germany:** East Berlin—Hans Becker, ADN, Zentralbild. **In France:** Paris—André Bénard, Odile Benoist, Elisabeth Bonhomme, Alain Degardin, Georges Delaleau, Gilbert Deloizy, Général Paul Dompnier, Deputy Director, Yvan Kayser, Général Pierre Lissarague, Director, Stéphane Nicolaou, Pierre Willefert, Curator, Musée de l'Air. **In Great Britain:** Cranwell—Mrs. J. M. King, Royal Air Force College; London—Denis Bateman, Royal Air Force, Air Historical Branch; Andrew Boyle; T. Charman, E. Hine, J. Lucas, G. Pavey, J. Simmons, M. Willis, Imperial War Museum; Ministry of Defence (Royal Air Force); R. W. Mack, P. Merton, Alison Uppard, Royal Air Force Museum. **In**

Italy: Milan—Giorgio Apostolo, Aerofan; Maurizio Pagliano; Rome—Contessa Maria Fede Caproni, Museo Aeronautico Caproni di Taliedo; Oscar Iandriani; General Domenico Ludovico (Ret.); General Ercole Savi (Ret.); Colonel Roberto Gasperini, Ufficio Propaganda, Maresciallo Ampelio Zanetti, Stato Maggiore Aeronautica. **In Japan:** Tokyo—Rokuro Konishi; Tadashi Nozawa; Kazuo Ohyauchi; Toyohashi—Fumio Iwaya; Yokohama—Shinkichi Natori. **In the Netherlands:** Amsterdam—Institute of Social History: Hilversum—Martin De Vries. **In the Union of Soviet Socialist Republics:** Moscow—Moscow House of Aviation and Cosmonautics; Photokhronika-TASS. **In the United States:** Alabama—Lieutenant Colonel John F. Guilmartin, Air University Review; California—Gabriel Jackson, University of California at San Diego; Connecticut—Harvey Lippincott, UTC Archives; Washington, D.C.—Jerry Kearns, John Kelly, Annette Melville, Library of Congress; Von Hardesty, Robert Mikesh, C. Glenn Sweeting, Robert van der Linden, National Air and Space Museum; Alice Price, The Pentagon; Maryland—

Richard S. Hallion, University of Maryland; Michigan—Don Gillmore; Nebraska—Edward L. Homze, University of Nebraska; Virginia—Dana Bell, United States Air Force Depository; Colonel Sam Roberts, Air Force Office of Public Affairs, Magazines and Books. **In West Germany:** Bonn—General Adolf Galland (Ret.); Koblenz—Heinz Held, Meinrad Nilges, Bundesarchiv; Mainz—Karl Ries; Munich—Hans Ebert, Messerschmitt-Bölkow-Blohm, Archive; Rudolf Heinrich, Deutsches Museum; Regensburg—Kurt Schnittke; West Berlin—Dr. Roland Klemig, Heidi Klein, Bildarchiv Preussischer Kulturbesitz; Peter Petrick; Axel Schulz, Ullstein Bilderdienst. Particularly useful sources of information and quotations used in this volume were *Trenchard* by Andrew Boyle, Collins, 1962; *The Billy Mitchell Affair* by Burke Davis, copyright © 1967 by Burke Davis, reprinted by permission of Random House, Inc.; *The Luftwaffe: Its Rise and Fall* by Hauptmann Hermann (Hermann Steiner), G. P. Putnam's Sons, 1943; *The Rise of the Luftwaffe* by Herbert M. Mason Jr., Dial Press, 1973.

Bibliography

Books

Aders, Gebhard, *History of the German Night Fighter Force 1917-1945.* London: Jane's Publishing Company, 1979.

Agar, Herbert, *The Darkest Year: Britain Alone June 1940-June 1941.* Doubleday, 1973.

Airborne Operations: An Illustrated Encyclopedia of the Great Battles of Airborne Forces. Crescent Books, 1979.

Allen, H. R.:
The Legacy of Lord Trenchard. London: Cassell & Company, 1972.
The Pegasus Book of Air Warfare. London: Dennis Dobson, 1968.

Angelucci, Enzo, and Paolo Matricardi, *World War II Airplanes,* Vols. 1 and 2. Rand McNally, 1978.

Arnold, H. H., *Global Mission.* Harper & Brothers, 1949.

Balbo, Italo, *My Air Armada.* London: Hurst & Blackett, 1934.

Baring, Maurice, *Flying Corps Headquarters 1914-1918.* London: William Blackwood & Sons, 1968.

Bell, Dana, *Air Force Colors Vol. I 1926-1942.* Squadron/Signal Publications, 1979.

Bender, Roger J., and George A. Peterson, *"Hermann Göring": From Regiment to Fallschirmpanzerkorps.* R. James Bender, 1975.

Bergamini, David, *Japan's Imperial Conspiracy,* Vols. 1 and 2. William Morrow and Company, 1971.

Black, Adam, *The R.A.F. in Action.* Macmillan, 1941.

Boyd, Alexander, *The Soviet Air Force Since 1918.* Stein and Day, 1977.

Boyle, Andrew, *Trenchard.* London: Collins, 1962.

Brown, David, Christopher Shores and Kenneth Macksey, *The Guinness History of Air Warfare.* Enfield: Guinness Superlatives Limited, 1976.

Brown, Eric, *Wings of the Luftwaffe: Flying German Aircraft of the Second World War.*

Doubleday, 1978.

Butler, Ewan, and Gordon Young, *Marshal without Glory.* London: Hodder & Stoughton, 1951.

Campbell, Christy, ed., *Naval Aircraft 1939-1945.* Chartwell Books, 1977.

Cappelluti, Frank J., "The Life and Thought of Giulio Douhet." Dissertation, Rutgers University, 1967.

Collier, Basil:
A History of Air Power. Macmillan, 1974.
Japanese Aircraft of World War II. Mayflower Books, 1979.

Cuny, Jean, *L'Aviation de chasse Française 1918-1940.* Éditions Lariviere, 1973.

Danel, Raymond, *L'Aviation Française de Bombardement et de Renseignement (1918/1940).* Éditions Lariviere, 1978.

Davis, Burke, *The Billy Mitchell Affair.* Random House, 1967.

Dicorato, Giuseppe, and Gianfranco Rotondi, *Storia dell'Aviazione.* Instituto Geografico De Agostini, 1978.

Douglas, Sholto, *Combat and Command: The Story of an Airman in Two World Wars.* Simon and Schuster, 1966.

Douhet, Giulio, *The Command of the Air.* Coward-McCann, 1942.

Duke, Neville, and Edward Lanchbery, eds., *The Crowded Sky: An Anthology of Flight from the Beginning to the Age of the Guided Missile.* London: Cassell & Company, 1959.

Dupuy, Trevor N., *The War in the Air.* Franklin Watts, 1976.

Ebert, Hans J., *Messerschmitt Bolkow Blohm: 111 MBB-Flugzeuge 1913-1978.* Stuttgart: Motorbuch Verlag, 1974.

Ellis, Paul, ed., *Aircraft of the RAF: A Pictorial Record 1918-1978.* London: Macdonald and Jane's, 1979.

Emme, Eugene M.:
The Impact of Air Power: National Security and World Politics. Van Nostrand, 1959.

Two Hundred Years of Flight in America: A Bicentennial Survey, Vol. I. American Astronautical Society, 1977.

Erickson, John, *The Soviet High Command: A Military-Political History.* St. Martin's Press, 1962.

Eyermann, Karl-Heinz, *Die Luftfahrt der UdSSr 1917-1977.* Berlin: Transpress, 1977.

Faber, Harold, ed., *Luftwaffe: A History.* Times Books, 1977.

Feist, Uwe, *Luftwaffe in World War II,* Part II. Aero Publishers, 1979.

Feist, Uwe, and René J. Francillon, *Luftwaffe in World War II.* Aero Publishers, 1968.

Fitzsimons, Bernard, *Warplanes & Air Battles of World War I.* Beekman House, 1973.

Flugel, Raymond R., *United States Air Power Doctrine: A Study of the Influence of William Mitchell and Giulio Douhet at the Air Corps Tactical School, 1921-1935.* Dissertation, University of Oklahoma, 1965.

Foundations of Air Power. United States Government Printing Office, 1958.

Francillon, René J., *Japanese Aircraft of the Pacific War.* London: Putnam, 1979.

Fraser, Ronald, *Blood of Spain: An Oral History of the Spanish Civil War.* Pantheon Books, 1979.

Frischauer, Willi, *Goering.* London: Odhams Press Limited, 1951.

Futrell, Robert F., *Ideas, Concepts, Doctrine: A History of Basic Thinking in the United States Air Force 1907-1964.* Air University, 1971.

Galland, Adolf, *The First and the Last: The German Fighter Force in World War II.* London: Methuen, 1955.

Gauvreau, Emile, and Lester Cohen, *Billy Mitchell: Founder of Our Air Force and Prophet without Honor.* E. P. Dutton, 1942.

Gibbs-Smith, Charles H., *Aviation: An Historical Survey from its Origins to the End of World War II.* London: Her Majesty's Stationery Office, 1970.

Glines, Carroll V., Jr., *The Compact History of the United States Air Force.* Hawthorn Books, 1973.

Goering, Emmy, *My Life with Goering.* London: David Bruce & Watson, 1972.

Goldberg, Alfred, ed., *A History of the United States Air Force 1907-1957.* Van Nostrand, 1957.

Graham, Frank, ed., *The Book of the XV Brigade.* New Castle: Frank Graham, 1975.

Green, William, *The Warplanes of the Third Reich.* Doubleday, 1970.

Grey, C. G.:
Bombers. London: Faber & Faber, 1941.
The Luftwaffe. London: Faber & Faber, 1944.

Gribble, Leonard R., *Epics of the Fighting R.A.F.* George G. Harrap, 1943.

Halley, James J., *The Role of the Fighter in Air Warfare.* Ziff-Davis Flying Books, 1978.

Heimann, Erich I I., *Die Flugzeuge der deutschen Lufthansa.* Stuttgart: Motorbuch Verlag, 1980.

Heinemann, Edward H., and Rosario Rausa, *Ed Heinemann: Combat Aircraft Designer.* Naval Institute Press, 1980.

Held, Werner, *Fighter! Luftwaffe Fighter Planes and Pilots.* London: Arms & Armour Press, 1979.

Hermann, Hauptmann, *The Luftwaffe: Its Rise and Fall.* G. P. Putnam's Sons, 1943.

Higham, Robin, *Air Power: A Concise History.* St. Martin's Press, 1972.

Homze, Edward L., *Arming the Luftwaffe: The Reich Air Ministry and the German Aircraft Industry 1919-1939.* University of Nebraska Press, 1976.

Hurley, Alfred F.:
The Aeronautical Ideas of General William Mitchell. Dissertation, Princeton University, 1961.
Billy Mitchell: Crusader for Air Power. Franklin Watts, Inc., 1964. New edition, Indiana University Press, 1975.

Hurley, Alfred F., and Robert C. Ehrhart, eds., *Air Power and Warfare.* United States Government Printing Office, 1979.

Irving, David, *The Rise and Fall of the Luftwaffe: The Life of Field Marshal Erhard Milch.* Little, Brown, 1973.

Jablonski, Edward:
Flying Fortress: The Illustrated Biography of the B-17s and the Men Who Flew Them. Doubleday, 1968.
Man with Wings: A Pictorial History of Aviation. Doubleday, 1980.

Jackson, A. J., *British Civil Aircraft Since 1919,* Vol. 1. London: Putnam, 1960.

Jackson, Gabriel, *The Spanish Republic and the Civil War 1931-1939.* Princeton University Press, 1965.

Jackson, Robert, *The Red Falcons: The Soviet Air Force in Action, 1919-1969.* London: Clifton Books, 1970.

James, A. G. Trevenen, *The Royal Air Force: The Past 30 Years.* London: Macdonald and Jane's, 1976.

Jane, Fred T.:
Jane's All the World's Aircraft 1919. Ed. and comp. by C. G. Grey. Arco, 1919.
Jane's All the World's Aircraft 1938. Comp. and ed. by C. G. Grey and Leonard Bridgman. Arco, 1938.

Jones, H. A., *The War in the Air: Being the Story of the Part Played in the Great War by the Roy-*

al Air Force. Oxford: Clarendon Press, 1937.

Jones, Lloyd S., *U.S. Fighters.* Aero Publishers, 1975.

Kilmarx, Robert A., *A History of Soviet Air Power.* London: Faber and Faber, 1962.

King, H. F., *Armament of British Aircraft 1909-1939.* London: Putnam, 1971.

Kohri, Katsu, Ikuo Komori and Ichiro Naito, *The Fifty Years of Japanese Aviation 1910-1960.* Tokyo: Kantosha Co., 1961.

Krauskopf, Robert W., *French Air Power Policy 1919-1939.* Dissertation, Georgetown University, 1965.

Larios, José, *Combat Over Spain.* Macmillan, 1966.

Lee, Asher:
The German Air Force. Harper & Brothers, 1946.
Goering: Air Leader. Hippocrene Books, 1972.
The Soviet Air Force. John Day, 1962.

Lee, Asher, ed., *The Soviet Air and Rocket Forces.* Frederick A. Praeger, 1959.

Levine, Isaac Don, *Mitchell: Pioneer of Air Power.* Duell, Sloan and Pearce, 1958.

Lewis, Peter, *The British Bomber Since 1914: Fifty Years of Design and Development.* Aero Publishers, 1967.

Mason, Herbert M., Jr., *The Rise of the Luftwaffe: Forging the Secret German Air Weapon 1918-1940.* Dial Press, 1973.

Miller, Nathan, *The Naval Air War 1939-1945.* The Nautical & Aviation Publishing Company of America, 1980.

Miller, Ronald, and David Sawers, *The Technical Development of Modern Aviation.* Praeger Publishers, 1970.

Mitchell, Ruth, *My Brother Bill: The Life of General "Billy" Mitchell.* Harcourt, Brace, 1953.

Mosley, Leonard, *The Reich Marshal: A Biography of Hermann Goering.* Doubleday, 1974.

Munson, Kenneth:
Boeing: An Aircraft Album No. 4. Arco, 1971.
Bombers Between the Wars 1919-39. Macmillan, 1970.
Bombers 1939-45. Macmillan, 1969.
Famous Aircraft of All Time. Arco, 1977.
Fighters Between the Wars 1919-39. Macmillan, 1970.
Fighters 1939-45. Macmillan, 1969.

Nielsen, Andreas, *The German Air Force General Staff.* Arno Press, 1968.

Norman, Aaron, *The Great Air War.* Macmillan, 1968.

Nowarra, Heinz J.:
Die Verbotenen Flugzeuge 1921-1935. Stuttgart: Motorbuch Verlag, 1980.
The Messerschmitt 109: A Famous German Fighter. Aero Publishers, 1963.

Nowarra, Heinz J., and G. R. Duval, *Russian Civil and Military Aircraft 1884-1969.* London: Fountain Press, 1970.

Plocher, Hermann, *The German Air Force in the Spanish War (1936-1939).* Manuscript, no date.

Potter, John D., *Yamamoto: The Man Who Menaced America.* Viking Press, 1965.

Price, Alfred:
The Bomber in World War II. London: Macdonald and Jane's, 1976.
Spitfire: A Documentary History. London: Macdonald and Jane's, 1977.

Progress in Aircraft Design Since 1903. U.S. Government Printing Office, 1978.

Roseberry, C. R., *The Challenging Skies: The Colorful Story of Aviation's Most Exciting Years 1919-1939.* Doubleday, 1966.

The Royal Air Force. London: Wm. Collins Sons, 1940.

Salas Larrazabal, Jesus, *Air War Over Spain.* London: Ian Allan, 1974.

Saundby, Robert, *Air Bombardment: The Story of its Development.* London: Chatto & Windus, 1961.

Saunders, Hilary St. George, *Per Ardua: The Rise of British Air Power 1911-1939.* Oxford University Press, 1945.

Schliephake, Hanfried, *The Birth of the Luftwaffe.* Henry Regnery, 1971.

Sekigawa, Eiichiro, *Pictorial History of Japanese Military Aviation.* London: Ian Allan, 1974.

Shores, Christopher, *Spanish Civil War Air Forces.* London: Osprey Publishing, 1977.

Sims, Charles, *The Royal Air Force: The First Fifty Years.* London: Adam & Charles Black, 1968.

Smith, J. R., and Anthony L. Kay, *German Aircraft of the Second World War.* London: Putnam, 1972.

Snyder, Louis L., *Encyclopedia of the Third Reich.* McGraw-Hill, 1976.

Spaight, J. M., *The Sky's The Limit: A Study of British Air Power.* London: Hodder and Stoughton, 1940.

Steer, G. L., *The Tree of Gernika: A Field Study of Modern War.* London: Hodder and Stoughton, 1938.

Stockwell, Richard E., *Soviet Air Power.* Pageant Press, 1956.

Suchenwirth, Richard:
The Development of the German Air Force, 1919-1939. Arno Press, 1970.
Command and Leadership in the German Air Force. USAF Historical Division, 1969.

Swanborough, F. G., *United States Military Aircraft Since 1909.* Putnam, 1963.

Tantum, W. H., IV and E. J. Hoffschmidt, *The Rise and Fall of the German Air Force (1933 to 1945).* WE, Inc., 1969.

Taylor, Telford, *Munich: The Price of Peace.* Doubleday, 1979.

Thomas, Gordon, and Max Morgan Witts, *Guernica: The Crucible of World War II.* Stein and Day, 1975.

Thomas, Hugh, *The Spanish Civil War.* Harper & Row, 1977.

Thompson, Jonathan W., *Italian Civil and Military Aircraft 1930-1945.* Aero Publishers, 1963.

Tinker, F. G., *Some Still Live: Experiences of a Fighting-plane Pilot in the Spanish War.* London: Lovat Dickson, 1938.

Van Haute, André, *Pictorial History of the French Air Force, Volume 1 1909-1949.* London: Ian Allan, 1974.

Wachtel, Joachim, *Lufthansa.* Cologne: Lufthansa German Airlines, 1975.

Ward, Richard, comp., *Hawker Hurricane MK.1/IV In Royal Air Force & Foreign Service.* Arco, 1971.

Wood, Derek, and Derek Dempster, *The Narrow Margin: The Battle of Britain and the Rise of Air Power 1930-40.* McGraw-Hill, 1969.

Yakovlev, A. S., *Fifty Years of Soviet Aircraft Construction.* Jerusalem: Israel Program for Scientific Translations, 1970.

Periodicals

Coox, Alvin D., "Restraints on Air Power in Limit-

ed War: Japan Vs. USSR At Chankufeng, 1938," *Aerospace Historian,* December 1970.
Emme, Eugene M.:
"The Genesis of Nazi Luftpolitik," *Air Power Historian,* January 1959.
"The Renaissance of German Air Power 1919-1932," *Air Power Historian,* July 1958.
Finick, Eugene, "I Fly for Spain," *Harpers,*

January 1938.
Guilmartin, John F., Jr., "Aspects of Airpower in the Spanish Civil War," *Air Power Historian,* April 1962.
Herr, Allen, "American Pilots in the Spanish Civil War," *Journal American Aviation Historical Society,* fall, 1977.
Proctor, Raymond, "They Flew from Pollensa

Bay," *Aerospace Historian,* December 1977.
Salas Larrazabal, Jesus, "Guernica: el Mito y la Realidad," *Revista de Aeronautica Y Astronautica,* August 1977.
Takamatsu, H., "Japanese Military Airplanes," *Aero Digest,* May 1933.
Young, Kennedy, "Wings of the Rising Sun," *Aero Digest,* December 1925.

Picture credits

Index